# INSIDE

# INSIDE
# GROUPS

## A PRACTICAL
## GUIDE TO
## ENCOUNTER
## GROUPS
## AND
## GROUP
## THERAPY

### Thomas R. Verny, M.D.

**McGraw-Hill Book Company**

New York • St. Louis • San Francisco • Düsseldorf • Mexico • Montreal

Panama • Paris • São Paulo • Tokyo • Toronto

Library of Congress Cataloging in Publication Data

Verny, Thomas R.
  Inside groups.

  Bibliography: p.
  1. Group relations training. 2. Group psychotherapy. I. Title.
HM 134.V47          158′.2          73-10392
ISBN 0-07-067407-8

First McGraw-Hill Paperback Edition, 1975

  2 3 4 5 6 7 8 9  MU MU  7 9 8 7 6 5

# Contents

# Introduction

**1**

With the tremendous mushrooming of growth groups from coast to coast and the great disparity in the styles and qualifications of group leaders, the public understandably has been deluged with wildly contradictory reports about these "new groups." While some former participants extol the virtues of their group experiences with a fervor bordering on religious ecstasy, others tell tales of horror reminiscent of medieval tortures. Even the politicians have been heard from. Those of the "right" speak of a communist plot and those of the "left" accuse the encounter group movement of harboring fascist ideas.

I hope in the following pages to strike a balance between an objective assessment of what these groups are all about and how they function and a subjective expression of my own feelings about their strengths and shortcomings. I have sought to write a practical, straightforward guide for those who wish to find out about the different approaches to groups and how to derive the most benefit from a group once they have joined it. After reading this book, those who have never been to a T-group, encounter group, or therapy group should be able to select the one most suited to their particular needs; and persons who are presently attending a group should gain a more thorough understanding of the intricacies of the group process and how to master it. I also hope my observations will benefit those people who have had a discouraging experience in groups—rekindling their interest and leading to more productive results. Finally, I would like to think that even group leaders and aspiring group leaders will find many ideas in this book that will stimulate their thinking.

Too many people either join groups for the wrong reasons or join the wrong groups for the right reasons. Others try to get "bootleg" therapy by participating in one weekend group after another instead of admitting to themselves that they really require psychotherapy on a regular basis. Most encounter group participants never get to see their leader before their session starts. They know nothing of him— sometimes not even his name. I shall therefore discuss how to select both a group and a group leader that are right for you. I shall also prepare you for the language of groups and the way they think. Groups have a culture all their own, and before you can fully benefit from one you have to learn the rules of the game. For example, most group therapy patients take from three to six months to become acclimated to the group, which represents a totally unnecessary loss of time and money to the patient. Hopefully, the following chapters will at least cut in half this "softening up" period. Prospective group members will thus be adequately prepared for the experience and better able to benefit from it.

One last word. Since this is neither a textbook nor a technical work, I have assumed that the reader has no special knowledge of psychology or its allied disciplines. I have tried to eliminate the clichés of the helping professions and to make these pages both informative and easy to understand.

# The Intimate
# Revolution

**II**

We can trace the present boom in self-awareness and "now" oriented groups to three major developments in the areas of psychiatry and psychology.

## Freud, the Unconscious, and Group Therapy

Sigmund Freud published his first paper discussing the unconscious in 1894. In this and his succeeding papers, books, and lectures, he advanced a theory for understanding the functioning of the mind and a method (free association, dream interpretation, etc.) for treating emotionally induced diseases of the mind and body. Very few psychoanalysts today practice orthodox psychoanalysis, and the majority of psychiatrists and psychologists use nonanalytic techniques.

Nonetheless, Freud's major concepts have withstood the test of time and are still accepted as valid.

With the exception of the behavior-modification therapies, the practice of individual and group therapy is based on the theoretical constructs of Freud and his followers. The term "group therapy" was first used by J. L. Moreno in 1920 in Vienna. In 1925 Moreno emigrated to the United States and introduced the concepts of "pyschodrama" and "sociodrama." (I will enlarge on these and subsequent terms in chapter VII, on group techniques.) S. R. Slavson and others began to use "activity group therapy" for children and adolescents in the thirties, and in the mid-forties Maxwell Jones started popularizing the concept of the therapeutic community and milieu therapy. Some of the insights derived from the field of group dynamics extended to the social structure of the world and even to the hospital.

As a result of the work of these men and countless others, group therapy became an established form of psychiatric treatment in the 1950s. Significantly, however, it was rarely considered the treatment of choice by either the profession or the laity. Psychiatrists, under the influence of their medical school training and traditional psychoanalytic theory, felt much more comfortable in a one-to-one relationship. Similarly, patients, reared in a society that prizes specialization and individuality, were reluctant to trust their feelings to a "bunch of strangers" instead of to the man in the white coat. Consequently, group therapy was widely used in places like mental hospitals or psychiatric out-patient clinics more because of expediency than choice. (It was the only way to cope with large numbers of people who otherwise would have gone totally untreated.) And, of course, there was little status connnected with being either a group therapist or a patient.

In the 1960s group therapy became revitalized by the contributions of Fritz Perls' *Gestalt Therapy,* a book published in 1951 but not taken seriously until a decade later. At approximately the same time, Eric Berne, with his *Transactional Analysis in Psychotherapy* (1961) and *Games People Play* (1964), and Alexander Lowen, author of *Love and Orgasm* and *The Betrayal of the Body,* reawakened interest in Wilhelm Reich's use of the body in analytic therapy. Lowen refers to his particular approach as "bioenergetic analysis." Each of these schools shares a common emphasis on here-and-now feelings—that is, feelings generated within the group—as opposed to anthropological expeditions into the past in search of psychic traumas. Each claims that the new experiential type of group therapy is much more exciting and more productive of deep personality changes than the traditional approach.

You can get a glimpse of how groups function one evening when you have some friends over. Suppose you notice a person tapping his foot, or making a fist while talking, or using the same word repeatedly in the course of the evening. If you point out this trait to him, you might witness an immediate change in the atmosphere of the group. Suddenly people will sit up and start listening. What was a dull evening might well become a serious exchange among people who, perhaps gingerly at first, will eventually begin to open up to each other. Once you experience a dialogue type of interchange, you will appreciate both the exhilaration of saying to someone something that you have wanted to say for a long time but did not dare and the danger (in this case minor) of the snowballing effect of emotionality carrying you to a never-never land from which you may have difficulty finding your way back without a guide.

If the stress on here and now is augmented by the judicious use of techniques from encounter, psychodrama, gestalt, etc., two hours of group therapy can give members enough to think about for the rest of the week. Unless otherwise stated, further discussions of group therapy in these pages will refer to this new experiential type of group therapy, which integrates knowledge gained from traditional individual and group therapy, from encounter groups, and from T-groups.

# Lewin, T-groups and Sensitivity Training

In the summer of 1946 Kurt Lewin asked three other prominent psychologists—K. Benne, L. Bradford, and Ronald Lippitt—to train a group of community leaders to implement more effectively the Connecticut Fair Employment Practices Act. All three had experience working on projects involving education and community relations. As part of the program, feedback sessions were set up during which lab assistants reported their observations to the research team. When the group members observed these sessions Bradford noted, "I remember very vividly the tremendous electric charge that took place as people reacted to data about their own behavior.[1] In 1947 sixty-seven participants and thirty-seven staff members gathered at the Gould Academy in Bethel, Maine, to explore new ways of learning about group processes and themselves (in that order). The term "T-group" (basic skill training group) was coined the following year.

[1] Louis A. Gottschalk, and E. Maxwell, "Psychiatric Perspectives on T-groups and the Laboratory Movement," *American Journal of Psychiatry,* December 1969, vol. 126, p. 823.

The National Training Laboratories (NTL) were formed in 1949 under the auspices of the National Education Association. (The word "laboratory" is used to convey both the experimental nature of the process and the importance placed on scientific methodology and observation.) Participants at NTL usually spend a week or longer in a residential workshop discussing a wide variety of subjects, with emphasis on communications. Participants come from many fields—particularly from government, private industry, religious organizations, and mental health disciplines—and while at NTL, they have a varied agenda. In recent years they have developed greatly from the original T-group, which focused on the members' interpersonal relationships, and NTL's work now embraces group dynamics, organizational development, and community development. Their new title is the NTL Institute for Applied Behavioral Science. As their activities have expanded, they have increasingly become involved in consultation and contract work in the planning of social change as well as laboratory training for managers and executives. Because of their emphasis on structural activities and their didactic orientation, NTLs are often most attractive to professional people. In fact, schools of education, business, and government represent the major sources of institutional and professional support.

During the past seventeen years, training laboratories have been established all over the United States. NTL currently employs over sixty-five full-time professional and administrative staff and has a network of six hundred NTL-trained group leaders. Whereas the Eastern labs have remained rather conservative, their primary forcus being communication in the group, group processes, and organizational goals, the West Coast labs have gradually come to stress personal growth. Labs of the latter type, often referred to as sensitivity training, overlap in their aims and functions, both with encounter and therapy groups. Following my discussion of the origins and present status of encounter groups, I will try to differentiate more among these three.

# Esalen Institute and the Encounter Group Movement

Most students of the encounter group movement date its origins back to 1961, when Michael Murphy and Richard Price took over Big Sur Hot Springs and established the Esalen Institute. Michael Murphy is typical of many encounter group devotees. Born in 1930 in Salinas, a stone's throw from San Francisco, his father was an attorney and his grandfather, who had purchased Big Sur Hot Springs in 1910, was a medical doctor. In his second year at Stanford University Murphy studied comparative religion; he says this course changed his whole life. He began to study Integral Yoga and to meditate and decided to become celibate. In 1956 after earning a B.A. in psychology, he went to Sri Aurobindo's ashram in India, where he stayed for eighteen months. Rasa Gustaitis in *Turning On* describes Murphy's impressions:

> This was a very interesting experimental community, attempting to combine the ideal of self-realization and technology, drawing upon Eastern spirituality and Western thought. The emphasis was on the transformation of your personal life into the divine nature—in our language, trying to evoke higher spiritual possibilities out of all your life.

After his return to San Francisco, Murphy met Richard Price, who, like himself, was searching for a more meaningful way to live than that offered by a career in academic psychology. In the fall of 1962 they held their first seminar, entitled "The Expanding Vision." Thus began an ever-expanding program of lectures, seminars, and workshops, often conducted by scholars such as Alan Watts, noted interpreter of Zen, Abraham Maslow and Carl Rogers, generally regarded as the theoretical fathers of the Human Potential Movement, and Paul Tillich, the influential Protestant theologian.

Esalen's aims and programs are set forth in the Institute's literature. Early in their development, in the September 1965 calendar, for example, it was stated:

> New tools and techniques of the human potentiality— generally unknown to the public and much of the intellectual community—are already at hand; many more are presently under development. We stand on an exhilarating and dangerous frontier, and must answer anew the old questions: What are the limits of human ability, the boundaries of human experience? What does it mean to be a human being?

And in the 1970s, a typical catalog offers the following list of programs:

a) San Francisco Single Evening Events:
   Rollo May: The Structure of Spiritual Experience
   Stanislav Grof: The Empire of LSD, etc.
b) San Francisco Workshops and Seminars:
   Joel Fort: Police and Revolutionaries
c) One-Day Workshops:
   Gordon Clough: Function of Philosophy in Psychological Experience; Weekend Seminar, etc.
d) Big Sur Workshops and Seminars:
   Richard Horan: Massage, Meditation, Yoga

e) Seven-Day Workshop:
   Tom and Natalie Ednie: Gestalt Open Workshop for
   Couples; Weekend Workshop, etc.
f) Big Sur Four-Week Program:
   Frederick Perls and Staff: Gestalt Open Professional
   Bernard Gunther and Staff: Body Awareness, etc.

During its first decade, the Esalen Program attracted considerable attention. In one year alone, 1967, four thousand people visited the Institute. Of these, seven hundred were psychologists and twenty-two decided to take a nine-month resident fellowship program in the various techniques developed at Esalen. Today Esalen program brochures are sent to approximately twenty-four thousand subscribers every year.

The Institute's success encouraged the development of similar centers, first across the United States and then in Canada, England, Europe, and Israel. They became drugless turn-on centers and referred to themselves as "growth centers." At present there are more than 150 in the United States.

But it was not the scientists, writers, theologians, or mystics who really captured the imagination of the public and put Esalen on the map. The Institute's fame was due primarily to the efforts of three people: Fritz Perls, William Schutz, and Bernard Gunther.

Fritz Perls was trained as a psychoanalyst. He spent World War II in South Africa and eventually settled in San Francisco. From 1964 to 1969 he conducted workshops and seminars in Gestalt therapy at Esalen. Shortly before his death, he moved to Vancouver to set up a Gestalt Institute in the form of a therapeutic community.

Although Perls was becoming known in professional circles in the late 1950s, only after he came to Esalen did he begin to make a real impact on interested lay people and mental health professionals alike. His direct, no-nonsense approach, his insistence on here-and-now feelings, and his employment of innovative techniques acted as a magnet to hundreds of students of Gestalt therapy. It was Perls' genius to forge a conceptual framework for Gestalt therapy out of some of the extremely complex theories of Kurt Goldstein, a neurologist in the 1920s, regarding the psychology of perception and the often equally abstruse formulations of existential psychiatry. In Perls a charismatic presence coalesced with a definite, easily understood approach to solving intrapsychic problems. He enjoyed playing the role of the guru, the elder statesman at Esalen, and his interactions with people who, as he put it, wanted "to work" on a problem were frequently funny or sad but almost always dramatic.

Perls has had a tremendous influence on the encounter movement and modern psychotherapy. His books—*Ego, Hunger, and Aggression, Gestalt Therapy, Gestalt Therapy Verbatim,* and *In and Out the Garbage Pail*—set forth his ideas and methods in detail. All of them (particularly the third) provide worthwhile reading.

Two of Gestalt therapy's favorite ploys are the "two chair" technique and to "play the projection." Each is aimed at making the unconscious conscious.

The "two chair" technique is particularly applicable to dream work. Although a strong interpretive element runs through all their therapeutic interventions Gestaltists avoid the word "interpretation." They feel that the patient should draw his own conclusions from his own experience. Once again you can see how much in tune this approach is with contemporary cultural norms—"Don't lay your trip on me, man." By not presuming to tell his patient what is going on in his head—which traditional therapies do—the Gestalt therapist expresses respect for the uniqueness of the individual and allows him to grow at his own pace.

Let us assume that a person dreamt that someone came up

from behind him and threatened him with a knife. In Gestalt therapy this individual would be asked to relate the dream as if it were actually happening: "I am standing in this large, dimly lit room; I am wearing jeans and a sweater; I smell candles burning," etc. When, in his narration the speaker reaches the point of describing the threat behind him, he would be asked to switch chairs, sit in the empty chair, and be the threatening person. Patients are told, "write a script" for the other person. This way a dialogue develops which allows the patient to integrate various aspects of his personality. The person who either naturally or by training can master this technique often achieves major insights or at least emotional catharsis in a matter of minutes. Since this is done in the presence of a group, it has the effect of encouraging others to take the plunge.

To "play the projection" is based on the assumption that most statements that people make regarding each other are projections. For example, patient says to therapist, "What you really mean is that you don't like me." At this point the Gestalt therapist may ask the patient to play the role of the therapist, who he feels does not like him. Or the patient may be asked to enact this attitude of not being likable. Either way he will discover for himself the conflicts he has in this area. Whereas Gestalt therapy is experiential but primarily verbal, the techniques developed by Schutz and Gunther place more stress on nonverbal ways of getting in touch with oneself.

Both men came to Esalen several years after Perls and from very diverse backgrounds. Bill Schutz received his Ph.D. in psychology in 1954, served on the Harvard faculty until 1958, and later was with the University of California at Berkeley. He acted as consultant for various private and government organizations and was involved in a number of extensive research projects involving small-group dynamics.

Gradually he moved away from what was essentially an NTL orientation to a more freewheeling encounter style which eventually brought him to Esalen. His book, *Joy,* subtitled *Expanding Human Awareness,* was, like Eric Berne's *Games People Play,* an instant best-seller. Here for the first time one could read, as the cover of *Joy* puts it somewhat breathlessly, how through "group games and the interplay of physical and mental self-revelation, new psychological insights are discovered."

Schutz is particularly strong on physical-contact games and group fantasies. For example, suppose two people in a group are unable to resolve their hostile feelings toward one another. Schutz will suggest "the Press," that is, he asks the two to stand in the middle of the group and face each other. Then one of the combatants is instructed to put his hands on the other's shoulders and press him to the ground if possible. The other may cooperate or resist. After the person is flat on his back the "victor" offers to help him up. Again, the other man may choose to accept or reject this gesture. When this transaction is completed, roles are reversed and the whole thing is repeated. After both have had a go at it the participants and the group will discuss their reactions to the exercise.

Involving oneself physically, with one's whole body, allows real feelings to surface and replace the rationalizations that all of us have in abundance. Furthermore, some of these emotions and thoughts are so powerful that one cannot deny them as one can other people's observations or interpretations. Many of these "structured interventions"—which is the elegant way of saying games, exercises, or techniques— have the same relationship to orthodox psychotherapeutic approaches as Zen has to Buddhism. They are powerful shorcuts to enlightenment.

About six hundred years ago a famous Zen master was

asked by a monk, "Please show me the essence of Zen." The Master replied, "Look under your feet!" In other words, the Master

> actualized satori by way of occupied space. The Zen man who has testified to the truth of self-nature lives in the realm where time and space are one . . . the true Zen man is the master of time and space living at the absolute spot of "here-now."[2]

The searchers for truth at Esalen—in fact, all those who like you and me are seeking to live more vitally and more meaningfully—may be using different approaches, but the process and the aims are the same as they have been for thousands of years. According to D. T. Suzuki, even the Buddha found it difficult to realize satori. The story goes that

> When he wished to be liberated from the bondage of birth and death he began to study philosophy, but this did not avail him, so he turned to asceticism. This made him so weak that he could not move, so he took milk and decided to go on with his search for liberation. Reasoning did not do any good and pursuing moral perfection did not help him either. Yet the urge to solve this problem was still there. He could go no farther, yet he could not retreat, so he had to stay where he was, but even that would not do. This state of spiritual crisis means that you cannot go on, nor retreat, nor stay where you are. When this dilemma is genuine, there prevails a state of consciousness ready for satori. When we really come to this stage (but we frequently think that what is not real is real), when we find ourselves at this critical moment, something is sure to rise from the depths of reality, from the depths of our own

---

[2] Abbott Zenkei Shibayama, *A Flower Does Not Talk*, Charles E. Tuttle Co., Rutland, Vermont, 1970.

being. When this comes up there is satori. Then you understand all things and are at peace with the world as well as with yourself.[3]

Another representative example from Schutz's repertoire of techniques is the introduction of a guided fantasy. Schutz will suggest to one or all members of the group simultaneously that they take a trip through their bodies. They are to enter their bodies by whatever orifice they wish and exit in any way they like. The emphasis is on making the experience as real as possible by trying to see, touch, smell, hear, etc., the way through one's system. Often two or three in a group will have quite extraordinary journeys. I recall one lady who entered her body through her vagina and within a few seconds turned into a rat chewing away at herself. Naturally, when she came back from this nightmare it provided us with a lot of material with which to investigate her sexual identity, sexual relations, and related problems.

Bernard Gunther, with a background in physical education, focuses even more than Schutz on body awareness. Gunther took LSD for three years as part of a research project. He studied Yoga and Zen and started reading Gestalt therapy. Then he met Charlotte Selver, a pioneer in sensory awareness, and took instruction from her for two years. Eventually, Gunther became a resident staff member at Esalen, where he perfected many of the techniques that are now so widely used throughout the world. He has collected these in a beautifully illustrated book, *Sense Relaxation,* which I recommend most highly. In this volume, which he calls "a book of experiments in being alive," Gunther attempts through the use of various techniques to integrate thinking and feeling more fully.

[3] D. T. Suzuki, *The Field of Zen,* Harper and Row, New York, 1970, p. 27.

The problem of language:
nouns and verbs.
The actor
separate from the action.
I injured my finger
rather than just hurting.
Being the observer
rather than the experience.
There is no static aspect
of the self;
but thinking makes it seem so.
This hoax,
this commonly accepted fantasy
is a division
that starts the basic split;
within the mind ego
are all of the different aspects
of you: the good you,
the bad you,
the should you, the have you.
Endless talk, magic words
about reality
become realer than what is real,
until you are able to stop
and realize
you're only all
one self.[4]

[4] Bernard Gunther, *Sense Relaxation*, Collier-Macmillan Canada Ltd., (Toronto, Ontario: 1969) p. 59.

# Getting Your Head in the Right Space

The questions most frequently asked by those who have either heard of or participated in growth groups are, "Just what are the differences among the various new groups? How do T-groups differ from encounter groups? Where does group psychotherapy fit in? What is sensitivity training?" In the preceding pages we have looked at the new groups from an historical perspective. Now I will discuss them from a more practical standpoint.

First, we must realize that none of these groups any longer exist in their pure, unadulterated form. During the last twenty years, particularly through professional publications and meetings, there has been a steady exchange of information among the three major "schools." Professionals trained as group therapists have moved into the encounter group field, while nonprofessionals doing encounter work often teach a T-group leader some encounter techniques. Much of the cross-fertilization is done also by participants. For example, a person who, after attending an encounter group, decides that he really needs more help with his problems may join an ongoing therapy group. In his therapy group sooner or later he will probably suggest the use of some of the techniques he was exposed to in his previous group.

Despite some degree of overlapping among these groups, however, major differences can still be delineated.

# Group Goals

*T-groups*, sensitivity training, human relations training, and the laboratory method all refer to group activities that are fundamentally educational in nature. They help men and women to examine their own behavior and their ways of relating to others and to learn from the experience. A spin-off of the T-group approach is organizational development (O.D.). Using knowledge and techniques from the behavioral sciences, O.D. attempts to integrate individual needs for growth and development with organizational goals and objectives.

NTL and related organizations are interested in providing consultative services not only to private industry but to a wide variety of community groups, family agencies, educational institutions, and government departments. The 1971 NTL Program announcement states: "It [NTL] works toward keeping change from becoming chaos by promoting flexibility and innovation and by providing help in planning. NTL offers no blueprint for the future, but does give leadership in developing alternatives and making choices. An NTL founding principle was and is to serve as a focal agency in developing the laboratory method of learning group dynamics."

*Encounter groups,* personal growth groups, the encounter group movement, and the human potential movement are interchangeable terms. Esalen Institute, the mother of growth centers, describes itself as "a center to explore those trends in the behavioral sciences, religion and philosophy which emphasize the potentialities and values of human existence. Its activities consist of seminars and workshops, . . . research and consulting programs, and a residential program exploring new directions in education and the behavioral sciences."

*Group therapy* goals are more ambitious and in a sense more difficult to achieve than those set by T-groups or encounter groups. Group therapy seeks to rid the patient of his symptoms (ulcers, depressions, frigidity); to increase his awareness and help him to control such self-defeating life patterns as anti-authoritarian attitudes, which cause him frequent job losses, and attachments to the "wrong" girls; to bring his intellect and his emotions into a better balance, thus enabling him to express anger or affection, or to avoid overanalyzing everything and feeling nothing; to help him to relate better to people; to immunize him as much as possible against further illness; in sum, to help him to develop into the kind of person he would like to be.

A lot of people incorrectly think the goal of psychotherapy is to make patients well adjusted. Good therapists (I shall discuss later how to select a good therapist, an encounter group, etc.) do not impose their own way of life on their patients. Rather, the object of therapy is to help the patient understand who he is, how he came to be the kind of person he is, and what he is willing to do to change (if this is what he wants).

So, where do you as an individual go from here?

If you desire to become more aware of the impact you make on others, if you wish to learn more about yourself and the way you communicate, or if you are concerned about interpersonal relations in business or other organizations, a T-group is a good first experience.

If you regard yourself as a person who has more than his share of hangups, plus or minus classical psychiatric symptoms, then you should consider joining a therapy group.

As a third alternative, if you are a person who feels fairly comfortable within his own skin and have done some reading about encounter groups (and perhaps even have known a friend who has participated in one), you may want to further your personal growth by joining an encounter group.

As you read on about the differences among these groups, keep comparing your goals and your personality needs with the goals and methods of the various groups, so that you can intelligently decide which kind of group is best suited for you.

# Institutional Affiliation of Groups

Some groups work within various university departments, others are associated with Y.M.C.A.s, and still others operate as part of their own network.

*NTL,* formerly allied with the National Education Association, has its head office in Arlington, Va., and has five regional offices throughout the United States. All its "trainers" have to meet high academic standards and must have passed a rigorous training program at NTL. Many Y.M.C.A.

programs and schools of business administration have followed the NTL model. Their focus is on executive development and the more humane and effective functioning of organizations. Although the laboratory movement had primarily an educational thrust at the beginning, only a minority of schools of education participate widely in NTL-type labs.

*T-groups* are often part of a management training course offered by large networks such as NTL, Y.M.C.A.s, or specialized personnel consultant firms. Frequently, they take place in specially designed conference centers or in hotels or motels. There is usually a certain convention air about these meetings, a mixture of earnestness and laxity. All sessions begin at the prescribed time, people bring paper and pencil with which to make notes, and a lot of mimeographed copies of what was done during the day are distributed. At night a great deal of drinking takes place since the participants are almost exclusively men who share the social world of business and government.

*Encounter groups* are usually conducted by the staff of a growth center. There are about a hundred and fifty of these centers across the United States and Canada. Some, such as Esalen, charge very high fees, receive grants, and just barely manage to survive financially. Others are small operations run by a few friends or even a family. For instance, a center at Strathmere, Ontario, states: "The centre of the community is an old stone house with resources of spacious rooms, books, tapes and records. . . . It offers long or short term residential opportunities which combine work, living with others and personal discovery experiences."

Some of the growth centers offer workshops which are accredited by an increasing number of universities. Thus, Esalen, in collaboration with several universities in California, offers courses leading to a master of arts degree or a doctor of philosophy or psychology degree. Further evidence of the growing maturity of the Human Potential Movement is the formation by the Association for Humanistic Psychology of the Humanistic Psychology Institute (H.P.I.). H.P.I. offers an M.A. and a Ph.D. degree in psychology in association with Sonoma State College.

One can see, then, the beginnings of the professionalization of encounter group leadership. Since this is a long-term development, the novice participant can do nothing at present but thoroughly research the growth center's affiliation, background, standards for staff acceptance, etc. The more university or other institutional affiliations the center has, the safer it is for a beginner. Most of all, be wary of the individual entrepreneur. He or she may be totally unqualified and a reject of the local growth center. (More about this when we discuss group leaders.)

In the case of *group psychotherapy* the situation is quite the opposite. Hardly any meaningful and innovative group work is done at the university, university-affiliated mental hospitals, or mental health clinics. The reasons for this are twofold.

First, these places usually deal with people who are either chronically ill or in the lower socioeconomic ranks. A person whose illness necessitates hospitalization is usually, and quite naturally, concerned only with getting rid of his symptoms and returning home as soon as possible. He is not interested in a year of group therapy. Consequently the treatment of both acute and chronic emotionally disturbed patients usually focuses on relief of symptoms through the use of tranquilizers or antidepressants and in some cases electroconvulsive treatments (ECT, more widely known as shock treatments). These, together with rest, occupational therapy, recreational therapy, sheltered workshops, and superficial forms of group therapy, represent by and large the treatment offered by the average psychiatric facility.

Secondly, group therapy is of a low caliber in institutions designed for the mentally ill because it is usually conducted either by resident psychiatrists (i.e., students) and/or paramedical personnel, such as nurses, physiotherapists, social workers, or psychology students.

In other words, you have a combination of poorly motivated patients and poorly trained staff. There are exceptions, but the fact remains that a good group therapy program is rarely found within the confines of a social agency, a church organization, or a mental health institution. Generally, the most competent group therapists are in private practice.

## The Group Leader

The most important factor in the group experience is the group leader. I describe my ideal group leader in chapter VI, on "the perfect patient" and "the perfect therapist." Right now I shall briefly discuss some of the major differences in leadership that exist among psychotherapy groups, encounter groups, and T-groups.

The role of the leader is most clearly defined in a *psychotherapy group.* Here a licensed mental health professional—a psychiatrist, psychologist, or social worker—assumes responsibility for helping his patients (in the case of a doctor) or his clients to feel better. Even the nonmedical practitioners follow an essentially medical model according to which someone who is in pain seeks relief by consulting a socially sanctioned healer.

One of the problems of this approach is its authoritarian

structure. In a situation where the leader views himself and is perceived by others as holding the key to life's secrets, it is very difficult for these "others" to mature and develop their full potential. The onus is always on the leader to do things for "me"—the patient, the helpless one.

Another common difficulty one encounters when dealing with orthodox, psychoanalytically oriented practitioners is their stress on the negative, destructive, immature characteristics or tendencies in one's personality to the exclusion of the positive and creative traits. Psychiatric terminology often tends to ascribe basically evil connotations to people's thoughts and actions. For example, schizophrenics, manic-depressives, and psychopaths are regarded as undesirable patients in terms of treatment; hysterical behavior or impulsive acting out are deemed undesirable forms of behavior. Many practitioners like to think that they operate in a value-free climate and do not pass judgment on their patients. This is simply not true. The great advantage of the medical model is that the practitioner is a person who has undergone anywhere from five to twelve years of university education and on-the-job supervision. Any person who has successfully completed his M.S.W., Ph.D., or M.D., plus several years of post-graduate work to obtain his specialist standing is at least capable of goal-directed behavior and long-term commitment. Having dedicated so much of his life to becoming what he is, the therapist is very much concerned to practice at a high level of competence. The chances are that he likes his profession. His motivations for—let us say—becoming a psychiatrist have been severely tested, and he has stood his ground in the face of many difficulties. This shows some stability of character and a willingness to assume responsibility. Furthermore, upon graduation he is answerable for his conduct to a professional body that has the power to revoke his license to practice.

Many *encounter group* leaders, on the other hand, are nonprofessionals and not answerable to anyone. For example, Jorge Rosner, who founded The Gestalt Institute of Toronto in the fall of 1972, has had one year of university education. Still, he studied Raja Yoga, was a student of Fritz Perls, was founder of the Theatre of Being in Chicago, and served as training director for Trans World Airlines. Bernard Gunther, as I noted earlier, studied to be a physical education teacher, received a B.A. in psychology, and then became involved in Esalen. Many growth centers, as well as NTL workshops, do not bother to mention who will conduct a particular group. They simply say "The Arica Staff" or "NTL Staff," expecting you to trust them implicitly. Personally, I would not like to be defended in court by the staff of "Your Friendly Neighborhood Legal Firm" or have my gall bladder removed by the staff of "Sharp Scalpel General Hospital." I would similarly be concerned about having my head handled by Growth Expert X.

Encounter group leaders come from many walks of life. They usually have an anti-intellectual, anti-academic bias, they have often undergone a chaotic period in their personal lives, traveled a fair bit, and been through a couple of marriages and various forms of psychotherapy. Because of their past, they place a high value on risk-taking behavior and personal freedom. Some of them tend to overemphasize this cult of personal freedom in their groups to the point of refusing to assume responsibility for anything that happens in the group. "I cannot make you do anything or feel anything that you don't want to," is their common refrain. This of course is a lot of nonsense. If I unexpectedly trip you as you come down the stairs your fall will hardly be a self-motivated act. Analogous situations on an emotional level abound in groups particularly when the focus is on nonverbal exercises.

A research study conducted by Stanford psychiatrist Irvin Yalom and University of Chicago psychologist Morton Lieberman revealed that leader style, not ideological approach, seemed to influence the rate of casualties in encounter groups. According to Yalom, "aggressive stimulators," that is, the charismatic, impatient, challenging, authoritarian leaders, headed the five groups which produced almost half the casualties. The authors do not tell us whether or not participants selected their own leaders—an important fact, for in my experience the sickest people tend to gravitate toward the sickest leaders. Under the guise of encounter or T-groups, these people really want a magic cure for what ails them. Therefore, they look for a magician, and when no magic or not enough magic occurs they get terribly disappointed, depressed, or even psychotic.

Encounter group leaders by and large are more directive than either psychotherapists or T-group facilitators. They also participate more in the group than the other two. Some encounter group leaders are into health foods, E.S.P., mysticism, and occultism—so if someone claims you have auras around your head, "beware!" Others tend to sexualize their relationships. Obviously, if you enter a group, keep your eyes open and take nothing for granted. If conventional mental health professionals bore you to death and you are not an organization man, you will most likely relate well to an encounter-oriented leader. I say "encounter-oriented" because today many health professionals and T-group leaders admit to this type of orientation.

*The T-group* trainer is usually described as a facilitator and a catalyst. Some trainers see themselves primarily as resource persons who establish the external structure within which self-development can occur. Often trainers will not start a group. Rather, they will sit with the assembled group members in a predetermined meeting place and just wait for someone to take the initiative. This is, paradoxically, a very active sort of passivity, because it is a very strong personality indeed who can withstand the demands of the group for direction and leadership. "Well, if you are not going to tell us what to do—what are you here for?" is a frequent response to this nondirective, authority-denying approach. Of course, the more the trainer refuses to act his expected role the more of a problem he becomes for the group.

At this point a split frequently occurs in the group. Some members will want to set up an executive committee with a president or chairman, a secretary, etc., and a definite agenda. Others will be more interested in looking at what is happening in the group right now. This is ordinarily the time the trainer starts helping the group to identify some of the issues, examine the options that are open to them, and begin to focus on the interactions in the group. Trainers are usually Rogerian in their outlook, that is, they tend to paraphrase what is said in such a way as to hold a mirror to the person so that he can see himself more objectively.

T-group trainers usually discuss the goals of each exercise with the participants prior to the exercise and provide some sort of closure at the end. The *Manual for Self-Development Workshops* offers the following advice to trainers:

> Avoid telling a person that he is "shy," "withdrawn," "pleasant," "obnoxious," etc. . . . For example, "shy," "withdrawn" could be stated as, "Some of the comments seem to indicate to me that people feel you don't participate as much in the conversations and discussions and are not as outspoken as you might be and that you tend to kind of pull into some kind of a shell sometimes and not say what you're thinking."[5]

[5] Robert C. Dorn, Peter Murdoch, & Alton T. Scarsborough, Jr. The Smith Richardson Foundation, 1970.

This kind of talk is fairly typical of trainers, counselors (especially teachers), clergymen, and social workers who have learned their craft on little old ladies with flowers and fruit on their hats. I really don't think that people in the 1970s are quite that fragile. The best that I can personally say about this gentle and wordy approach is that it does no harm. Once again please keep in mind that this is the extreme T-group facilitator position and that your average trainer will most likely be more directive and more real.

Clearly, if you are a present or future consumer of mental health services, you need to check out your "healer's" assumptions about the healing process. This applies not only to group therapy but also to individual therapy, T-groups, encounter groups, etc. There are still too many people who, overly impressed by the degrees or the fame and reputation of their guru, deliver themselves into his hands with no questions asked. There is nothing mystical or shameful about going to a "shrink" or social worker or counselor of any sort. However, you are contracting for a service and you are entitled to know what you will receive in return for your time and money.

# Participants and Styles of Participation

*T-group* participants usually come from large private or public organizations. Since the average six-day workshop costs $500, most individuals who attend are sent by their companies or by government agencies who pay their way. Organizations sometimes exert a subtle pressure on their executives to attend. For example, a vice president of a certain firm attends a lab on "Creativity in Organizations" and thinks it was terrific. So on his return he approaches an executive of his company who he feels has not been working as well as in previous years and suggests that the executive go to the same lab next year. The executive thus approached feels, quite rightly, that his vice president is being critical of his work. He is in no position to refuse, but because of his negative feelings toward the vice president he arrives at the lab quite hostile and unwilling to benefit from it. Indeed, until the source of his resentment is resolved in the group the chances are that he will not derive any benefit from attending.

The same can be said of anyone who is in a growth-producing situation against his will. If a man comes to see me for a consultation and I ask him, "Why are you here?" and he answers, "Because my wife thinks I need to see a psychiatrist," I know I have an uphill struggle before me.

Getting back to T-groups. The members of T-groups are usually successful middle-class professionals or businessmen. Even programs like "Teams for Campus Change" or "Institutional Racism: Its Practices and Alternatives" attract people who are achievement oriented. They are certainly the most emotionally stable of the three groups under discussion and the least psychologically sophisticated. Because the labs are largely publicized as an instrument of exploration and skill development rather than personal change, members are not prepared to look too deeply into themselves. The usual subjects of discussion are work situations, hobbies, children, and sometimes wives. (I say wives because the great majority of T-group members are men.)

Sessions often start with one of the facilitators discussing a particular subject for ten or fifteen minutes, answering questions about it, and providing a resource guide for further reading. Then exercises are introduced which focus on cooperation, competition, and self-evaluation. Many of the techniques used are paper and pencil exercises; thus any but the most civilized confrontations are avoided. The members are also supplied with a lot of printed material, which they file away in glossy folders with their names imprinted on them.

In contrast to T-group members, *group therapy* patients more or less readily identify themselves as "sick": They feel they are involved in repetitive self-damaging behavior to which they wish to put a stop. It is almost impossible to categorize group therapy members except in terms of the agency or individual mental health professional they seek out. Family service associations or mental health clinics usually have the patients no one else wants. On the other hand, private therapists select their patients carefully, building up a clientele which in time becomes self-perpetuating. Thus, Therapist X may offer analytically oriented therapy to older mental-health professionals, lawyers, dentists, etc. Therapist Y may practice Gestalt therapy and have a group of younger patients—students, teachers, nurses. Therapist Z may be into psychodrama and see mostly middle-aged housewives.

The two most common ways in which patients come into group therapy are through referral by a general practitioner, clergyman, or the like, or through friends who are or were patients. In the case of the former, most nonmental-health professionals really do not know what kind of therapy their favorite psychiatrist, psychologist, or social worker offers. They may know him personally and think that he is a nice guy, or one of their former referrals has done well and so they hope this one will do well too, or finally, the therapist is on the teaching staff of a large hospital and therefore "he must be good." Nonmental-health professionals are, unfortunately, just as confused by the wide variety of approaches to therapy as everybody else is, and they really have no way of knowing which method in the hands of which therapist will most benefit their prospective patient. There-

fore, when your gynecologist or lawyer or teacher or who-
ever urges you to see a psychiatrist, Dr. Shrink, ask him
why he thinks that this particular person would be more
helpful than another psychiatrist. You are entitled to know.
Your head is at stake.

I think a better way of finding out what goes on in a
therapist's office is through a friend who has been making
good progress for some time in Dr. Joe Psychologist's group.
He will tell you about the composition of the group, whether
it is slow- or fast-paced, and whether it is past- or here-and-
now oriented.

Although more women than men seek therapy, most
group leaders prefer to have an equal number of members
of each sex in the group. As a rule, the women are more aggressive than they would like to be, and the men are more
passive than they would like to be. In each group there are
some who, because of their verbal facility, dominate the
conversation and others who need to be asked a direct question before they can open their mouths. But more on this
later.

Group therapy participants tend to be well read and
to believe that talking to others about their problems will
increase their self-understanding and alleviate their difficulties. Because most of the writing in the area of pop-
psychology still stresses insight through verbal interchange,
group members often overintellectualize and shy away from
emotions.

*Encounter Group* participants, like group therapy patients,
are eager to learn how they function individually and in
groups. As a rule, they are younger than either group therapy or T-group members, more anti-intellectual and anti-
establishment in their views, and more body oriented. They
may come into the group with highly unrealistic expectations as a result of what they have heard or read about

groups. Mose encounter groups have no selection proce-
dure; therefore, you may end up in a group with a person
who is quite sick in the traditional psychiatric sense or who
is so angry his main object is to destroy the group. The
presence of one such person can ruin a group. If you should
run across one of these people who, for whatever reason,
constantly injects himself into the conversation, intimidates
psychologically, or threatens physically, do not hesitate to
eject him from the group. This is your group and you have
the right (as well as the obligation to yourself) to speak up
and to benefit as much as possible from this experience. One
of the cardinal precepts of the encounter culture is that risk
taking should be encouraged—and the sooner you start
taking risks, the better for you and the group.

What I have said about individual psychotherapists at-
tracting a certain clientele applies to a lesser degree to encounter groups. Participants who seek out Ida Rolf at Esalen
will be quite different from those signing up for John Lilly's
"The Human Biocomputer" two-week workshop.

The cost of a weekend encounter, plus room and board,
is about $95–$120; that of a five-day workshop is approximately $250.

# Group Structure and Techniques

*Encounter groups* usually take the form of a weekend re-
treat, lasting from Friday evening to Sunday afternoon. Participants number about fourteen to sixteen with a fairly even
female/male ratio. There is usually no follow-up. If the participant wants to get more of the same, he must attend another, similar group in the future.

The techniques used in encounter groups are primarily
those of verbal and nonverbal confrontation, psychodrama,

Gestalt, and sensory awareness. Many other approaches may also be utilized, such as fantasy, meditation, and transactional analysis. These techniques are, no doubt, one of the main reasons for the phenomenal popularity of encounter groups for they enable the participants to communicate on a level of honesty that they are not able to achieve even with old friends. The push for openness and self-revelation is very strong in such groups and contributes to the intensity of the experience. Many of the games used allow participants to get in touch with their child-ego states so that they can have temper tantrums or roll down the grassy slopes of a hill. The message of the techniques is simply, "it's all right to feel."

*T-groups* last from five days to two weeks. The group's size runs from ten to fourteen with a predominance of males. Some of the labs have follow-up meetings; all require a written application form.

In T-groups, thinking predominates over feeling, and concern for role functioning takes precedence over being. Thus, a lab entitled "New Ways of Teaching and Learning" (conducted at Bethel, Maine, in 1972) produced the following statement about techniques:

> Program activities center around simulation, gaming, role playing analysis of classroom experiences and interaction among the various participants in the learning process.
> . . . Participants will work in level clusters (elementary, secondary, higher) to examine common problems and specialize in areas appropriate to their professional roles.

A different kind of T-group, a "Basic Human Interaction Laboratory" seeks "to enable participants to generalize from their experiences. . . . Research information and knowledge from the behavioral sciences are supplied in various ways."

In contrast, *group therapy* sessions focus on the patients' problems and are basically role denying in nature. As in encounter groups, in group therapy the participants and the leader want to get to know you, and the way you really are, without such social armor as diplomas, degrees, or bank balances. Whether the group sessions deal with here-and-now feelings only, past experiences and dreams, everyday occurrences, or a mixture of all or some of these depends on the outlook of the particular therapist. Group therapy really works well when feelings run high—not an easy achievement on the basis of one two-and-a-half-hour meeting per week.

The group therapist who is humanistically oriented will concentrate on the multiple transferences of the members— that is, their feelings from the past projected onto people in the present who in some ways resemble past key people. He encourages the open expression of both positive and negative emotions, utilizing such methods as psychodrama, constructive techniques, and trust exercises.

Most therapists discourage patients from discussing their symptoms at length. This often strikes new pateints as very odd, since it was these very symptoms that prompted them to seek treatment. But therapists who take this tack know what they are doing. Headaches, ulcers, inability to sleep, fear of crossing the street, frigidity, impotence, or other symptoms, are just the outward manifestations of unresolved, unconscious conflicts. Only by resolving these conflicts will the symptoms disappear. You can resolve them by intellectually and emotionally experiencing and understanding them—healing comes about when the unconscious is made conscious. The task of therapy is to bring these unconscious conflicts into the open and to see the patient through the difficult period of adjustment. Because members often view the group as a family unit, it can serve as a source of constant encouragement to the person who is trying out new modes of behavior. In this sense a group can be much more effective than an individual therapist under the same circumstances.

Most therapy groups are open ended: When a patient is sufficiently recovered he terminates treatment and another patient takes his place in the group. The average length of stay of patients in a group is twelve to eighteen months. Avoid a group where people come and go as they please. In such an environment it is impossible to develop any lasting relationships, and without these you cannot have trust and honesty. The ideal group is one where every three to four months a few members leave because they are feeling better. This rotation of participants allows for both continuity and fresh blood. At the other end of the spectrum is the group that goes on and on with a membership change only when someone moves away, marries, or dies. Such groups satisfy the neurotic needs of the therapist who plays into the neurotic needs of his patients. They are not a vehicle for growth.

## Summing Up

If you are considering entering a group, keep in mind your personal goals and your life style and how these will mesh with those of the group you are about to join. Remember that none of the groups described can brainwash you, or make you into something you are not, or take something away from you—unless you want to have it taken away. But they can scare you or put you off for a long time unless you know what to expect. If you don't understand something or are not sure of the leader's approach, *ask!* Hopefully, with the information in this chapter you will be better equipped to ask relevant questions and thus will end up getting your head in the right space.

# Taking the Plunge

## IV

There are certain fears shared by most new members of a group, whether it is a T-group, encounter group, or even a ladies' auxiliary. People are afraid of not fitting in. They may think they are not as intelligent, as well educated, or as attractive looking as the rest of the members. Since a group usually represents a microcosm of humanity, the chances are very good that its members will evince the entire spectrum of human attributes. With a few exceptions!

The great majority of growth-group participants are white, middle class, well read, and of average or above-average intelligence. I have never yet met a truckdriver or a bricklayer in an encounter group. Similarly, large corporations may send their executives to a T-group but would disapprove of their attending an encounter group or therapy group. Most group leaders, if they have a say in the matter, tend to select young, bright, presentable people.

In the final analysis the group leader selects members

whom he likes. This "liking" is an indefinite composite of various feelings and thoughts that the leader gains from his assessment of the future participant. The motivation, psychological mindedness, and sophistication of the applicant may be all-important. Or "liking" might depend on the leader's theoretical interest in a particular person's problems, his past successes with analogous cases, and source of referral. Consequently, if you have had a personal interview with your therapist (please remember, I am using terms like therapist, group leader, and facilitator interchangeably) and he suggests that you should join a group, you can be fairly certain that he really wants you to be in his group.

Unfortunately, a lot of people still think of group therapy as a poor cousin to individual therapy. They may not admit as much when group therapy is first suggested to them, but they resent the idea nonetheless and will do so until their feelings are brought to light by the therapist or other group members. So if you think this way, don't sulk for months— talk about it!

Others, particularly those who are entering what they perceive to be a challenging, dynamic group, are afraid that they will be forced to participate in activities they may not be ready for or approve of. I must admit that a few leaders are more interested in seeing fireworks than real, honest—albeit sometimes plodding—progress. Also, you may encounter a few "career groupies" who have made the rounds, seen Berne and Lowen and Perls, and cannot differentiate between honesty and brutality. A responsible group leader will respect your position and will protect you against such sharks, but should you ever have to face them alone all you need to say is, "I hear what you are saying but I am not prepared to get into that right now." If the leader or the group persists, just tell them to "fuck off." A show of anger coupled with a four-letter word is often the quickest and most effective way to keep a group bully off your back.

Just remember: All the other members either are as new to the group as you are, or a short time ago were in your boots and therefore know how you feel.

A widespread fantasy of new patients is that they will have to reveal themselves to a jury composed of unsympathetic men and women who will try them, find them inadequate, and judge them guilty. In effect, they are afraid of being rejected. This fear, acquired in early childhood, is commonly triggered when a person finds himself in an unfamiliar situation. Only by repeatedly thrusting himself into such situations and making every attempt at resolving the causes of his fear can a man rid himself of this irrational attitude. The group is an ideal environment within which to grapple with this problem.

If you are going to benefit from a restructuring type of group or individual experience (encounter or therapy), you must learn to ride against your own fears. Your common sense will tell you not to reveal your defenses, yet the group ethic will pull you in the opposite direction. Everything in you will tell you to be nice and polite and not to make waves. This attitude is counterproductive to your goals, and the sooner you abandon it the sooner you will free yourself of your hangups.

Before discussing common maneuvers used by people to avoid making progress, we should look at two fears which fall in the gray area between "normal" anticipatory anxieties and resistance to change. The first—the contagion fantasy—is the dread of catching the sickness of the other group members, as if they all suffered from chickenpox or leprosy. The second is the fear of loss of control. It has many roots, for it is unconsciously associated with loss of bladder or bowel control, sexual orgasm, murderous rage, going insane, and dying.

On a deeper level—and you will find learning about yourself is not unlike peeling an onion—fear of loss of control, like all the other defenses of the  unconscious, is an anxiety-relieving mechanism that protects you against feeling hurt. Just as fever is the body's normal defense against an invasion by noxious agents such as germs or viruses, defense mechanisms serve a useful function up to a point. Unfortunately, the organism's temperature-regulating system sometimes gets out of control (for example, as a result of a brain tumor) and can actually cause death. Similarly, a person's defense mechanism may, instead of working for his emotional well-being, begin to work against his best interests. Many people become psychologically thwarted or damaged at an early age, and they carry this pain with them wherever they go. Their defenses act like the walls of an abscess, protecting the body against the pus but also not allowing the pus to be drained, or allowing for a slow, imperceptible seepage which gradually infects the surrounding tissues. Unless the pus is let out, the person can never be whole or free.

For these reasons, we must learn about our self-defeating behavior patterns and our inappropriate defensive operations—how they originated and what they are protecting. Only when we have plumbed the depths of our being can we begin to change. And that, in essence, is what self-awareness or growth or therapy at its best is all about.

# Common Defensive Ploys

People have numerous ways in which to protect themselves against feelings, whether these be positive, loving, caring feelings or negative, hostile, angry ones. They assume different defensive postures, and when one approach fails they always have another one to fall back upon. All neurotic, disconnected people are emotionally bent on finishing the unfinished business of the past. Their behavior patterns are an outward manifestation of this unconscious wish to feel whole again. The little girl who had a cold, intellectual father will spend all her life attaching herself to cold, intellectual men, hoping to warm them up so that she will finally get the love from them she wanted to get from her father. Of course, she has an uncanny ability to select men who turn out to be just like father and will not be able to give her what she wants. Or the little boy whose mother was always angry and abusive toward him will, when he grows up, attempt to provoke women into being angry and abusive toward him. This is the only type of woman he knows how to relate to. And he hopes that one day, after all that shit has been heaped on him, he will have earned the right to be loved.

The following is an actual transcript from one of my group therapy sessions. It demonstrates, I think rather well, how one particular person—Jean (all names of course are fictitious)—is constantly shifting ground in order not to become involved with the group and, ultimately, with her own feelings.

JEAN: I don't think we really care about each other at all. I mean I quite frankly don't care one shit about any of you and I don't care if any of you solve your problems. Right now all I care about is that I solve my problems and I don't care about you people because I don't know you as people.

HARRY: I believe that until you do start caring about the people here you will never improve because you will never learn to care about yourself.

JEAN: Why should I care about the people here? I was brought here and it is for me a completely foreign situation.

ART: Are you not here because you wanted to be here?

JEAN: Well yes, I thought it would help me but I just realized it won't.

HARRY: What do you mean, you've just realized now?

JEAN: I didn't just realize now—I realized it last week. I've been realizing it week by week by week . . .

HARRY: Actually you realized it the first week, didn't you? Your comment the first week was, "Well, basically this is it. I don't know whether the group will help me a lot and frankly I can't see how it can, but I'll give it a whirl." That was basically it.

JEAN: I don't know whether I realized it exactly . . .

PAULINE: You don't contribute in this group.

JEAN: Because I don't relate to a group. I cannot relate to a group easily and therefore it's a problem. I can't relate to a group socially. I mean, I can't, I don't feel comfortable in a group situation. You're all worried about getting through to them . . . I really don't want to be in group. I don't enjoy being in a group and I doubt if I ever will or want to be. You know, like I'll tolerate groups when I have to be in groups, and that's all—I don't really want to be in group.

HARRY: I think we ought not to try to pressure you into liking group. But I don't think you gave it a fair shake.

JEAN: No, maybe not.

HARRY: I don't know why you ever did stay here for six months.

JEAN: You want to know why I came here for so long? Because it was interesting to know that other people have problems too, and it was interesting to look into them, and it was interesting to hear how other people's minds work. But that's not going to help me anymore.

GAIL: The way people's minds work!

JEAN: Yes, the way people's minds work. What's wrong with that?

GAIL: That's so mechanical.

JEAN: Well that's the way I think of it.

GAIL: You don't leave yourself open enough in the group to be touched.

JEAN: There's a good reason for that, and that's because I feel very uncomfortable in a group.

HARRY: What is the difference between being here and being in the office alone with the therapist?

JEAN: There's a big difference to me; I don't know why. I guess I don't trust people. I mean I know it is something to do with my background and my upbringing—it's probably very simple really when you get down to it and I don't feel emotional, and going to group, I do feel emotional, but I don't trust people enough to let go with my emotions.

THERAPIST: You have said on previous occasions that you had trouble revealing yourself, your real feelings, to the group.

GEORGE: You've often made statements where you talk about yourself and you stand firm on your thinking and you are not willing to budge—you don't yield at all, you say, "No, I didn't. If I did say something else I didn't mean it, and this is what I mean." To me it seems you aren't receptive to anything anybody says, in other words, you've made up your mind as to what you are going to say and you want complete control over what anybody is saying to you. I guess this is very fundamental to group working, that is, if you can't accept what anybody is saying then there's no use in being in group.

JEAN: But that isn't true because I have occasionally asked people here what they thought of certain things in my personal life.

GEORGE: Tell me the areas in which you want the criticism to come, and the people you want to receive it from.

JEAN: All right, I'm saying that I can take criticism and that I will if I feel it is warranted.

PAM: But the minute somebody brings up trust or faith you clam up.

JEAN: I feel that I have to have an inner strength to keep going and one of the things that gives me the drive and the strength to keep on going with my life is the determination about what I'm doing.

GAIL: I remember a couple of months ago you came in and you said, "My foundations are getting very shaky." I think that's very basically where we are at.

JEAN: I know they are not secure; I'm trying to say that it is extremely difficult for me in the group situation to get anywhere.

GAIL: All I'm saying is that if your defenses are shaky, which they are, then you are not going to change it on your own.

JEAN: What makes you think that group will help me get rid of them? I've been brought up, which is something I realized this weekend, to be, to feel I must be independent and must never rely upon anybody else ever, for anything.

GEORGE: Do you think that by jumping group you will change that?

JEAN: I don't know whether jumping group, as you say, will help me. I would love to be able to relate here, I just find it extremely difficult. It's something, I . . . it's like a sort of wall, I just can't get through.

PAM: Try to overcome it. Because I went home the other day and thought about it and I felt quite a bit like you. If I can't make it in that group, how the hell am I going to make it in life? And that's why I wrote that letter and came back.

THERAPIST: Do you think it has been easier for you since you made up your mind?

PAM: It's still not easy, but I do feel much more part of the group.

MARION: You're just more, well, coming out, you know, you're not as reserved, you give more feedback.

JEAN: Most of the time that I am here, while another person talks I can't find a way of bringing up what I'm feeling. If I can't find a way of expressing it then how can I participate?

PAM: But if you said even that sometimes, it would help. Then we could start relating to you.

JEAN: Before I came to group I was very shy, very withdrawn . . . even the first couple of weeks I was in this group I was very quiet. . . . It hit me about two weeks ago that it was really hostile to sit, just sit here and not say anything.

GEORGE: You said that as a child you were always being forced to be independent, you were always leaving families and growing up on your own.

JEAN: Yes, but on the other hand, as soon as I got too independent, that's when all the hassles started.

GEORGE: In a way you're repeating the same pattern with us but in this case nobody is forcing you out, you're forcing yourself out.

JEAN: I feel like a driven person. I don't think that my trying to relate to people is going to change me.

GAIL: You said in your family, you were expected to be very independent. I find you extremely dependent. I think you are very dependent on your friends. I think you are very dependent on your boyfriend. I think in a sense you are very dependent on this group. But I think you also realize that we are not going to allow you to be dependent.

PAM: Maybe being dependent frightens you.

JEAN: You haven't told me why I ought to stay. I told you why I can't relate here, and you haven't told me anything to convince me to change my mind.

THERAPIST: Your comment of "Why I can't relate" is no different than person X, Y, or Z's problem of why I can't make it with women or why I always choose the wrong men or why I have the compulsion to wash my hands three times—it's a problem for which you need help. And it is one of those problems that you can work out right here. Why I have to wash my hands three times is difficult to deal with in a group. You can actually look at why it is that you and Harry, for example don't feel comfortable with each other. You can put that problem right here on the floor and look at it.

JEAN: But I don't, I don't. And I feel that there is not enough time.

THERAPIST: That's a lot of horse shit. There is always enough time for people. The point is that you have to face the fact that you really don't want to find out. You're kidding yourself. You're trying to live with the illusion that you really want to get to the bottom of it but you take one step forward and two steps back every time anybody comes even close to you. You can go on for the rest of your life changing groups and doing all sorts of things pretending that you are trying to help yourself, but you will not grow until you start digging deeper.

JEAN: I don't believe that. I really do want to help myself to get to the bottom of this.

PAM: Why don't you think about everything that was said here and not make a final decision tonight. Just think it over carefully.

JEAN: I feel that if I am going to talk here that my train of thought is going to be interrupted and somebody else is going to start talking and that I just feel that . . .

THERAPIST: . . . that you won't be able to control it.

JEAN: Also I feel that what I'm going to say just isn't worth saying compared to what somebody else is saying. And I'm not going to get any reaction to what I say.

THERAPIST: If you really don't want to be interrupted, all you have to say is "Look group, I want ten minutes to myself and I don't want any interruptions." The group will cooperate. It's all a matter of doing it instead of thinking about it. Putting up blocks of what might happen; and then they will do this, and then that and so I'm not going to do this.

JEAN: Well I've never thought of that.

THERAPIST: Isn't this the one place you shouldn't have to worry about what we think about you because . . .

JEAN: I don't care what you think about me. . . . It's that you're not going to pay enough attention to me.

THERAPIST: O.K. I would be interested in hearing from some of the other people. Dave, how do you feel about Jean?

DAVE [*to Jean*]: Why do you feel that there is something so horrible about yourself that people will not listen to you?

JEAN: Because I've been brought up to think that I'm horrible.

DAVE: Don't you think that perhaps the experience of people who care would correct that? I don't know you . . . but I don't think you are horrible.

THERAPIST: I think that you have come so far and that you will hit a wall and now you are at a point where you will either have to shit or get off the pot. You are afraid to talk because you might get rejected and you might also find out unpleasant things about yourself and then you would need to change. So it is easier for you to say "I am going to turn away and I'm not going to do it."

Jean subsequently decided to stay in therapy and made good progress from then on.

Many people have a tendency to relate to the group the way they related to their family. They will often react to the leader as a parental figure and to other members—or one particular member—as siblings. Becoming aware of these patterns and experiencing the feelings that go with them enables a person to reflect on his life and rediscover his true feelings about the key people in his past. You can see this happening when Jean said, "I've been brought up, which is something I realized this weekend, to be, to feel I must be independent and must never rely upon anybody else ever, for anything."

Pam, whom you have already met, wrote me the following two letters a few weeks before the above discussion with Jean.

Wednesday

Dear Tom:

I think only you really realize just how stressful a situation I have found group. I am rearing a baby racoon, and each time I go to feed her, she growls, fluffs up her coat and rapidly backs away from me, and I guess that is how I have found group. When I have gone in, I feel as though my autonomic nervous system really gets going. When I talk, I feel awful, and vulnerable and boring to the others, and when I don't, like today, I just build up resentment. I have honestly tried, and tried, to cope with the group situation, and have kept coming back, and trying again, and even now feel nothing but regret that I couldn't make it.

But I have learnt a lot from group, which people in my everyday life notice. I am calmer, happier, more able to cope with situations, gradually learning to express things more openly instead of harboring resentments. But still feel very "isolated."

So please don't be mad with me Tom. I have tried to cope with the group process, but I feel for me it is rather like learning to swim in the Atlantic ocean.

Pam

Friday

Dear Tom:

I have thought and thought. If I can't cope with criticism in the group, how will I ever really change.

I am talking out far more—finding that saying how I feel has not made my relationship with John "poisonous," like telling my parents, finding it really does clear the air.

I am writing this in the positive, because I am damned if I am going to say "Please, Tom, can I come back" but I would die if you had replaced me without me knowing.

Will it help if I take Valium for a while before group to stop me freezing up? Also, I do feel that you could give me some help on this.

Yours sincerely,

Pam

Here again you can clearly see the internal struggle between letting go of one's defenses and holding on to them.

Let us briefly look at some of the more florid ploys people use to shore up their defenses.

## FLIGHT

Flight may occur either very early in the life of a group or when the person begins to feel the validity of what others are saying to him and, as a result, becomes anxious.

I have known individuals who, after two or three group therapy sessions, would report to the group that the last few weeks had been a tremendously enriching experience, that they have never felt better, and that they see no further need for therapy. Don't believe it! These people are running scared, and it's the group's job to tell them so. (What they do with that information is, of course, their choice.)

Few growth experiences that meaningfully alters one's fundamental orientation in life can take place without some pain, anxiety, depression, and hostility. If you are in a group where everything is just sweetness and light and laughter and good comradeship, do not expect to find out significant things about yourself. This is not to say that you cannot have fun and good feelings in a group, but you must confront the darker side of human nature before you can achieve the goals you have set for yourself.


## YOU ARE VERY NICE BUT NOT MY TYPE

When a person joins a group he or she will often feel like an outsider. Even if all the other members are new and equally ill at ease, someone might say what a young lady said recently at an encounter group in order to justify her desire to quit after a few hours: "You are just not my type of people."

This is really only another form of taking flight. The chances are good that the people in your group are much like you, and even in the unlikely event that all the members are teenage drug addicts and you are a 45-year-old certified public accountant, your presence might prove to be a broadening experience. (Most group leaders would of course never put you into such a group.) Your belief that they are totally different from you is an expression of your self-protecting and self-defeating defense mechanisms and is, therefore, invalid.


## HOW DO I KNOW THAT I CAN TRUST YOU?

"People will find out that I am in group," or "You know one of my friends and she will now know everything about me." Here is a really far-out one: "One day my daughter may not be able to get married (she is four) because her boyfriend may be told what kind of a person his future mother-in-law really is."

All group members are concerned about confidentiality.

And rightly so. Unless what is said remains confidential you will have a tea party instead of a genuine encounter. Thus, the building up of mutual trust is a very important part of the life of the group. Every participant has a vested interest in keeping what happens in the group a secret. Frequently, references to confidentiality are an expression of a participant's painful experience with an important person in his childhood who he feels had let him down.

Individuals engage in a lot of projecting in the area of trust. This means that the person who is most adamant about keeping everything that happens confidential is often the very person who blabbers about the group the first opportunity he gets, or at least is tempted to do so but fights the urge. He sees or looks for in others what he tries not to recognize in himself.

Personally, I don't think that anyone should feel ashamed of attending a T-group, encounter group, or any form of therapy. Indeed, I have found that an almost direct relationship exists between the number of people who know a patient is in group therapy and the progress he makes in therapy. A man who is not certain whether he should tell his wife or his friends or his parents is usually uncertain about a lot of other things too, such as, "Should I be in therapy?" "Will this really work for me?" "Is today a good time to discuss my dreams?"

The more committed a person becomes to his own growth, the less attention he will pay to the opinion of others, and the more he will benefit from this experience. So, if you want a rough measure of how you are doing in group, count the number of people who know that you attend one. You get only half a point if you call it a "course," "lecture," or "workshop." Deduct a point if you call it a "dentist's appointment" or "visiting Aunt Millie, whose husband passed away."

## DELAYING TACTICS

Putting things off is a fairly widespread frailty of the human race, and, naturally, when anxiety-provoking situations are involved the temptation is great to procrastinate.

Some of the common refrains I hear are, "I was very low yesterday but today I feel fine," "I was too upset last week to come to group," "I feel too depressed right now to talk about it; perhaps, next time," "I've already taken up too much of the group's time; there must be others who want to talk" (just as she is about to explode).

All these people know that sooner or later they will have to come to terms with their feelings. But they never seem to feel strong enough to do it. In fact, "feeling low" will allow them to pierce their defensive armor more quickly. Therefore, instead of avoiding sensations, weakness, and vulnerability, they should seek out these feelings and make them work for them! Since the whole object of therapy is to break down the shell around people, it is pointless to come to therapy only when you are feeling fine or to speak only when one's emotions are well under control.

## NOBODY UNDERSTANDS ME

Thus speaks the eternal masochist, the person who enjoys receiving—and often meting out—punishment. There is always a cloud of doom and gloom hovering over these people. They can turn the happiest occasion into a disaster, a compliment into a criticism. And they always try—they try earnestly to apply for a job (but the alarm clock did not go off), to leave home (I cannot, it would kill mother), to stop drinking (too much pressure this week at work). Often they are full of aches and pains, and they will ask, "Are you sure, doctor, that this is all in my mind?" They would much prefer to have a fatal disease or at least a brain tumor.

No matter how much attention is paid to these sufferers, it is never enough. "I've spilled my guts out here and no one seems to care." If they actually were able to admit that some-one did care, they would have to change their whole way of conceptualizing reality, and, often, protestations to the contrary, they are not prepared to do that.

Such people have difficulty benefiting from a group. If things are not going well for them, if the other members eventually get fed up listening to their endless litany, their life-denying script is positively reinforced—"nobody loves me." Should they start changing in spite of themselves and should the group encourage change, they get scared and under some pretext bolt from the group.

## THE INTELLECTUALIZERS

Thinking one's feelings away is a favorite pastime of group members. When you consider the high premium that our society places on quick, rational thinking and the fact that a majority of group participants are bright, well-educated, successful people, it is not surprising that they overutilize their cognitive faculties.

The intellectualizer may appear in any of several guises. The "clarifier," for example asks all sorts of useful questions meant to help the person who is talking understand himself better. Like the "summarizer," he tells the group what the speaker has *really* been saying. Both the "clarifier" and the "summarizer" can give the impression that they are partici-pating in and contributing a lot to the group when in fact they only give the illusion of involvement and do not experience any deep feelings. Their constant questioning keeps someone else in the hot seat and gains them reprieve for another day from sitting in it themselves. The group has a tendency to be rather lenient with these people because they do keep the action going, particularly on slow days.

The "totally rational individual" never gets upset. He claims that the group is an artificial situation, that he would not select the people in the group for his friends if he had a chance and, consequently, that any similarity between the group situation and his life in the real world is purely coincidental. He knows we mean well even when we try to make him angry. He cannot produce feelings at command. Often the "totally rational individual" and the "scholar" are kindred spirits. The latter has a propensity for literary quotes, philosophical excursions, and political commentaries. Occasionally, the two may be quite entertaining. More frequently, their verbal virtuosity intimidates the less eloquent members of the group, and thus they tend to have a generally disruptive effect.

The "assistant therapist" usually has read more books on psychology, psychiatry, and encounter than the therapist and the rest of the group combined. He has a constant need to show off his knowledge. Group members often think that he was "planted" in the group by the therapist for some dark purpose. In cases where the group did not know the identity of the leader in their midst they have actually mistaken such a person for the leader. Unless the true leader moves in, the assistant therapist can quickly fall from his "exalted position" to that of the class scapegoat.

Similarly, the Florence Nightingale type, who rushes around from one needy person to another dispensing her own brand of good cheer and homespun advice, will rapidly be reminded, sometimes roughly, that the giving out of Band-Aids cannot take the place of real emotional involvement in the group.

## THE EXASPERATERS

These people really annoy the hell out of a group. They often arouse very strong resentment and then act surprised—like, "What did I do to deserve this?" Some of them play dumb: They never understand what is being said, they forget what they were asked three seconds ago, or they never remember what occurred last week. They also manage to contravene the simplest rules of the group (which have been spelled out again and again), such as no drinking before a session. "I really didn't know," they say with wide-eyed innocence.

Others play "polite." "I could not speak because Joe was speaking and I did not want to interrupt." Of course, it is not polite to interrupt, to get angry at someone, or even to cry in front of strangers. But you are not in group to be polite. You are there to get in touch with your true feelings—whatever they may be. So leave your social niceties and tact behind when you enter group.

A somewhat bewildering lot are the people who say, "I cannot come to group unless. . . ." You can fill in the blanks with, "I can take a tranquilizer or a shot of liquor beforehand," or "I can smoke during the session," or "I can sit on *that* chair." I don't think it is worth spending too much time on such people. Their motivation is so fragile and their grasp on reality so tenuous that unless they can make the adjustment and play by the rules, the group is better off without them.

I feel very strongly that no one should be courted or coerced into a group. There is a fine line between helping a man to reach further into his past or to stay longer in the group and actually forcing a person to do something that obviously he is not prepared to do. This is where the clinical acumen of the leader comes into play. He must know how far each person at any given time is ready to travel and not push him, or allow the group to push him, beyond that point.

After a protracted period in therapy some patients continue to attend, "just in case." To them group represents a form of health insurance, and as long as they come they will be okay. People like this are often useful for the therapist to have around. They know the ropes, they are good, loyal group members, and they often tell disheartened newer members how sick they were two years ago "and look at me now." The therapist sometimes forgets how long such people have been attending group because they are so nice and helpful.

On the other hand, because most of their problems have been solved, the just-in-case-I-should-get-sick-and-need-the-group-again patient does not contribute very much to the group and can thus become a source of tension. He also begins to feel "old" in the group; all his former buddies have left, and he feels kind of lonely. In such cases it is best to start working toward an early termination of therapy and assure the patient that, should he ever require help again, there will always be a spot for him in "his" group.

The "out-there" person is one who always relates things to the group which are of no general concern to anyone (including the speaker) and which have hardly any emotional valence attached to them. Consequently, in the long run, his colleagues can only react to these stories with scorn or irritation. Most members begin therapy with a there-and-then position, but quickly learn to shift their focus to issues and feelings in the immediate present in the group. The "out-there" person is a slow learner, and he gets a certain degree of satisfaction from the way he is able to stir things up.

The "confused" person is even more interested than the out-there person in controlling and manipulating the group. That is why the reaction to a person who adopts this role can sometimes be quite violent. The individual who acts confused is never able to make anything clear. For example, she will always be going in or just coming out of a crisis. Usually, there are two or more men in her life: one is nice, but she does not get turned on by him sexually; the other is a real bastard, and he is the one she wants. Often she is unemployed and has two or three children from previous affairs and marriages. When she talks about people and events it is rarely clear who she is referring to and when these events actually took place. Sometimes it is difficult to differentiate fact from fantasy from dreams in her narration.

The "confused" person is like one of those legendary dragons; everytime you cut off one of its heads, two grow out from the same place. The moment that the group succeeds in understanding and resolving one problem, it finds out that that was not a serious problem at all, but what the Confused one really wanted to talk about was. . . .

## THE SHIT DISTURBERS

These people are ahead of the intellectualizers—they are capable of feeling. Alas, their repertoire is limited to only one predominant emotion: ANGER.

The "shit disturbers" usually fall into two categories: the "attackers" and the "seducers." The behavior of the former covers the whole spectrum from mild hostility to open challenge to the leader. They might start by being picky about the furniture, the lighting, or the meal hours. They then go on to tell the group why it is not working properly and why it never will—under the present regime. I use the term "attackers" advisedly because many of these antagonists are young radical students, anti-authoritarian and anti-intellectual, who perceive the group leader as part of an oppressive bourgeois system which they are intent on destroying. They will make every possible attempt to sabotage the group process. Unfortunately, one such person is capable of destroying a weekend group if his needs are not met.

If you are one of these angry men or sulking women (you may wish to reverse the order of any of the above words in case you feel they are discriminatory against either sex), you should realize that the group is not a political arena. It is a place for getting your head together. You are free to pursue your political aims outside the group. Of course, if you are an out-and-out anarchist, Minuteman, or Maoist you will not listen to this suggestion—or probably, even open this book. So I can only address myself to your fellow group members and say that, although a group is a powerful tool for positive change, it does have its limitations.

The political activist would be the first to agree that the whole is more important than its parts—that ends justify means. Although I do not accept these generalizations, I do believe that occasions arise when the good of eight or ten individuals takes precedence over the good of one, especially if that one is determined not to benefit from the experience. In short, when everything else fails, do not spend the whole weekend pacifying an intellectually angry person. Unless he is willing to look at the real sources of his anger and interact with others in the group as human beings instead of as capitalists, workers, Jews, Blacks, Whiteys, etc., ask him, in no uncertain terms, to leave.

The "seducers" sexualize their anger. Some men exhibit their Betz cells (the fifth layer of large ganglion cells in the brain cortex, responsible for cognition) the way coquettish women cross their legs with everything but their navels showing. This is not a good way to attract attention, and the response the "seducers" elicit is not the one they desire. The girl with the plunging neckline will not be able to comprehend why so many men in the group treat her like a sexual object. The man who describes in great detail his latest sexual conquest will be surprised when women in the group are hesitant to accept a lift from him or have coffee with him after group.

The "seducers" must learn to unscramble their communications to the world and to the group. Sex is usually not what they want or need. Just as the openly hostile person, who really needs to be loved, must be denied the counter-hostility he seeks because he knows how to deal with it, so the seductive one must be denied sexual gratification in the group to insure his or her progress.

I mentioned at the beginning of this chapter that the group in many ways recreates the family situation for some people. It is only natural under these circumstances that some of the participants who have unfinished business with their brothers, sisters, mother, or father develop deep attachments to one of their fellow members or the group leader. These too can be a form of resistance, because, unless they are successfully solved, the person is stuck with powerful feelings he does not know how to handle. The first step toward resolution of such feelings is to be open about them.

I have seen many patients and some former group participants who quit a group because they were embarrassed to talk to their therapist about their loving feelings toward him. It is a sad comment on the way we are brought up that we have relatively little trouble getting angry at a person but we do not dare to show affection. (If these feelings are both loving and frankly lecherous, and if they should be reciprocated by the group leader, then it's an entirely different situation. I shall deal with this issue in the chapter on the ideal therapist.)

## THE GROUP ADDICT

This is a person who makes a career of going from group to group or therapist to therapist but never commits himself totally to any one approach. He shops around for the most recently popular "cure." While some people will save their money for a year to spend a week in Spain, the group addict will take his holidays at Esalen being Rolfed. Although there is much to be said in favor of the latter choice, doing it year after year is surely nonsensical. The eternal patient would really rather switch than change. His compulsive behavior fools no one but himself.

Admittedly, some methods are better than others, and certain group therapists are more knowledgeable than others. Yet to be unable to benefit significantly from a series of groups ought to convince this person that the fault may lie with him instead of with group A, B, C, or D.

## THE PREPSYCHOTIC

The prepsychotic is a person who is on the verge of a severe personality disorganization which may lead to a temporary or sometimes permanent loss of contact with reality. The individual who is afraid of going crazy hardly ever falls into this category. By and large prepsychotics tend to be withdrawn men or women who come to group because they are aware of their difficulties of relating to, and feeling like, other people.

Human beings become psychotic because, instead of letting their feelings out, they build bigger and stronger walls around themselves until the walls crumble and everything is swept aside by the damned-up pain. The group environment does act as a powerful catalyst for feelings. If the feelings are worked with as they are mobilized, then there is no problem. But if an individual continuously keeps shoving them under, the lid of his id might blow.

There is no reason why a group that is properly constituted, and where the level of trust is high, could not help an acutely disorganized and disoriented individual. Indeed, some people need to lose touch with reality temporarily before they can become totally integrated again. The leader who is not experienced in these matters should not endeavor to work with an individual who is likely to become psychotic. Most responsible therapists know their limitations and will act accordingly.

The following is an excerpt from an ongoing group where Al demonstrates many of the resistances I have discussed, particularly those of the "scholar" and the "shit disturbers."

AL: I never feel that anybody ever has enough information about the other person, and especially about me and my wife, to make certain suggestions as to how we should live together. I really resent that on the basis of insufficient information the psychiatrist or anybody else in the group makes suggestions which will deeply affect our lives. You see, you just don't seem to be able to understand that it's not possible for me to get really interested in, emotionally or in any other way, some of the bullshit that goes on in here, which I think is the biggest waste of time that I've ever seen, and for me not to respond emotionally, I consider to be the height of good sense and perfect sanity.

THERAPIST: Well then react intellectually, but react, instead of just sitting there being passive like a blob.

AL: I'm not passive, I just feel totally bored by some of the things that are going on here.

THERAPIST: Well then, why don't you interrupt?

AL: I don't do that probably because I'm not interested enough.

EVE: From my own experience, I've had times in the group when people asked me here, "Why don't you leave Eve?" This gives me a chance to think about what they're saying, it doesn't mean I have to listen to it. I don't think you can blame the group or the psychiatrist for asking Margie or even telling her what to do. In the final analysis it's still up to you.

AL: You're quite right, as far as that is concerned. That's not really what I'm angry about. I'm just using it as an example of what I don't like about this group. I'm tired of being told that I don't feel anything. I cannot bleed or get upset about some of the things that you people seem to find moving.

JEAN: Or perhaps Al is cold.

AL: Al is not cold; Al is cold when he is confronted by people who are so fucking boring as you are. Al does not strike the rest of his friends as cold and they are deeply feeling people.

JEAN: Too bad they aren't here.

NORM: I would like him to go on articulating what is the matter with the group. I don't want the group to attack him on each single point.

THERAPIST: You are saying that people here do not interest you, which is very different from saying that there's a lot of bullshit going on in the group.

AL: Well wait a minute now, just hold on a second; I was angry so I said that you were boring and stupid. All I meant to say was that you have problems that I cannot identify with; they go on and on and there's no progress made, and that bores me. I'm not uncomfortable with it,

I do not wish anybody harm, I just wish they would get on with it and get better.

THERAPIST: Well do you think that instead of just sitting there angry and frustrated, you could do something in a positive way to help these people?

AL: I don't think so; I've heard these people go on and on.

THERAPIST: Do you feel hopeless about it?

AL: Yes I do. The crux of the matter really, is I just don't think I have enough of a problem to be here. I'm probably taking up valuable space that somebody else could be using. I resist this, what I call democratization of emotions, that we all must feel the same way, which seems to be the prevailing mood in this group.

JEAN: Does it really not bother you, that every one of us here, can sit here and talk, and you are not interested in any one of us?

AL: No, not really.

HAROLD: One more thing Al. When you talk, all I hear is commentary and commentary; it's always commentary on something that's happened. Very little do we hear about what's going on with you now. I can't explain to you why, one has to experience it to really appreciate the difference between that and the commentary type of talk that you're doing most of the time.

AL: I have feelings, and just because you don't know about them, doesn't mean that they don't exist. Well look, doesn't it seem odd to you, that we are thrown together in the random arrangement of nine people, and just because of that situation, you really expect that you're going to end up caring very deeply for all these other nine people?

ANN: You're not feeling sad for personalities, you're feeling sad for the people as you get to know them, and the kinds of things that they stand for, and the kinds of things that they talk about. They're all human beings, and I start reaching to them as I get to know them as human beings.

AL: You're breaking my heart. That's the same thing as feeling deeply for the North Vietnamese, for Christ's sake.

ANN: It's different, because here you are exposed very closely and very intimately to nine other people for a prolonged period of time, and that's very different from the North Vietnamese.

AL: Well that's probably true, but I just don't feel it here. I don't want to be exposed to nine other personalities. Even if some of you here care because I'm in the group, that still does not make any difference to me, I'm tired of all the bleeding that goes on in here, and I think it's time for some clear thinking.

NORM: You know, Al, you really can't fault the group for making judgments on the basis of inadequate information. That's the structure of the group and you have to grope around. It's your prerogative to reject it or to fight it.

BOB: I feel closer to Al than to any other man in this group. I should deplore it greatly if he were to leave. As long as he's here, the group will not degenerate into a mutual admiration society.

AL: That makes me feel good enough to reconsider. I really think I need this kind of a group.

## Summing Up

This chapter has dealt with the kinds of fearful fantasies people commonly have on entering a group and the various ways in which they defend themselves against becoming involved in the group process. All of us share in these anxieties and protective mechanisms; it's only a matter of degree and how much we are willing to work at diminishing them that separates those of us who can get down to the nitty gritty and resolve our difficulties from those eternal fence-sitters who waste their lives running away from themselves.

# V

# Now Down to the Nitty-Gritty

It is crucial for a new participant to understand clearly what he wants to gain from his group experience. Unless a serious attempt is made by him to work out—first in his own head and then with his group leader—what his goals are, his chances of gaining significantly from the group are poor indeed. It is simply not enough to say, "I feel depressed," or "I feel alienated," or "I want to improve my marriage." The problem needs to be articulated and defined in such terms that the leader can in effect say, "Yes, this I can help you with, that I can't—perhaps you better see a behavior therapist or a primal therapist to resolve that problem." Remember that no one in the helping professions can read your mind. They can tell a lot about you in terms of levels of depression, anxiety, or muscle tension, but they cannot assess you adequately if you don't talk.

Many of my colleagues and I are repeatedly surprised (although we should know better by now) to discover how defensive people are when they seek help. Most people have such a neurotic obsession with being liked, even by total strangers whom they may never see again, that they will lie or omit unsavory details from their life histories—having had three abortions, for example—or embellish facts to make themselves look stronger or more successful. This camouflaging simply creates the wrong impression of you vis-a-vis the therapist and hampers your therapy. So come clean! Let your therapist know who you are and how you want to change. Then he will tell you whether or not your aims are realistic.

A facilitator or therapist who refuses to enter into this kind of contract with you should be avoided. The domain of faith is religion, not therapy. The leader who is not willing to be open with you and level with you is not together enough to be your guru. There are some leaders, particularly of psychoanalytic orientation, who firmly believe that not saying anything about themselves is beneficial to their groups. I am not advocating that you question the therapist about how he raises his children or whether he has a good sex life—although I think that these are valid questions—but I strongly believe that he must give you some idea of what he proposes to do with you, how long it will take, and how much it will cost.

As I discussed in chapter III, different groups vary in the length of time they require your attendance. Whatever that period may be, it is imperative that you attend consistently and for the whole duration of the session. In other words, if you have a party on Saturday night, you would be foolish to leave a weekend encounter group for that one evening and return on Sunday morning and expect to get the full benefit from the group. The other members would probably be very angry with you for deserting them. Many significant interchanges may have occurred in your absence, and there would just not be enough time to clue you in. In effect, you would be joining a new group when you returned on Sunday, and you would feel like a stranger. So do not underestimate the importance of missing one session, whether it be on a weekend encounter or in an ongoing weekly group.

If you are going to be absent or late, let the group know. It is unfair to them if they just sit around talking chickenshit while waiting for you. I have a rule in my groups: Anyone who misses three sessions in a three-month period without notification is asked to discontinue attendance permanently. If last session Mary got Bill very angry and Bill wants to discuss it today but Mary is not there, both of them have lost an opportunity. Two weeks later the feelings have cooled and they may not be activated again for a long time. Therefore, regularity of attendance in spite of colds and menstrual cramps and sun spots is worth the effort in the long run.

In the previous chapter I talked about individuals who do not come to group when they feel sad or anxious or suicidal. There are also people who avoid coming when they have a headache, menstrual cramps, or arthritic pains. My suggestion is: Bring your headache or any other aches and pains to the group; don't dull your senses with painkillers, tranquilizers, alcohol, or mood elevators. There is a reason why you feel the way you do; let's find out what it is. The same applies to smoking. People use cigarettes as a crutch; in group they light up when they are tense. This permits them to gain time, to compose themselves, to avoid feeling. Since we want to get at the root of the tension, not cover it up or delay exploring it for another week, I ask all my patients to desist from smoking during group therapy.

There are always some individuals who think that they cannot manage without a tranquilizer or a cigarette. I really believe that this is a cop-out and reflects their unwillingness to experience even a small degree of discomfort in the interest of change. Anyone who is not willing to do this or switch his bridge night to another night of the week or celebrate his wife's birthday on a different night (I know it comes once a year) is too poorly motivated to benefit from the group.

All these remarks are aimed at the new group member. However, sometimes when you are well into the life of the group you may notice that it is getting harder and harder for you to make that 5 o'clock appointment on Mondays. Either there is unfinished business on your desk, or the children seem to be crankier and need you more, or your mother is sick and you really ought to visit her today. You are up against some internal, unconscious resistance, and the sooner you bring it up in the group the sooner you can resolve it and achieve your stated objectives.

Termination is also a very important part of the contract. I ask all participants in my groups to agree, before joining the group, that should they feel at any point like quitting, they are free to do so as long as they confront the group with their decision. I do not want to get a telephone call or a letter saying something like, "Dr. Verny, you have been of great help but I will not be attending any more sessions. I think I can manage on my own." Whether a person is ending group because he is improved or because he is making insufficient progress, the other members, who have invested time and effort in this person, deserve to hear about it. Furthermore, people are often tempted to discontinue therapy because the group has stirred up anxiety in them and they do not wish to dwell on it further. They would rather suppress their feelings and cling to their neuroses.

Some of the most therapeutically profound experiences have occurred when a group member in his "last hour" opened up the floodgates and really let loose with his feelings. The group will not hold back an individual who is truly ready to leave. But it is usually successful in persuading a person who is just running away to stay and work through his problems.

## Head Talk/Gut Talk

Growth groups have a unique way of thinking and relating, as well as a language and an ethic of their own. It is sometimes difficult, therefore, for a neophyte to become a full-fledged member in good standing. The initiation rites, like all rites of passage, can be quite an ordeal—but they don't need to be.

No man or woman undergoes any kind of personality change just by understanding himself or herself better. The intellectual insight that "I am competitive because I had an older brother who preempted my parents' love" or "I like older women because I have an unresolved Oedipal attachment" makes good conversation for cocktail parties but does not contribute to any deep-seated psychic transformations.

The medicine men of old, the shamans, the revivalist preachers, the psychotherapists—all the professional helpers—have "cured" people by making them experience "feelings" strongly. An altered state of consciousness or a heightened sense of awareness (it does not matter what you call it) is brought about through the ritualistic use of incantations, music, drugs, fear, and expectations of great and magical occurrences, and, of course, by the words and touch of the healer and his assistants. This is the main reason why encounter group leaders, experiential group therapists, and others working in progressive ways with groups will insist that you talk about your feelings and not your thoughts.

Too much of what once passed under the guise of group therapy (and still does in some quarters) is now called "head talk." Some of you may have had the misfortune to be exposed to this type of group and know the scene—eight men and women sitting on chairs in a circle listening to how Mabel was beaten up again by her drunken husband. They all look interested and some are concerned. Some even make a few suggestions on how she should handle the situation. But Mabel finds fault with them all. Finally, she asks the therapist for advice. And he predictably answers, "Well, what do you think you should do?" After two hours everyone moves back to square one. It is truly a tribute to man's capacity to grow through contact with others that some patients have actually improved even in groups such as these.

The majority of new group members have difficulty grasping the difference between "head talk" and "gut talk." I ask them, "What are you feeling right now?" "I am thinking of tomorrow's test." "That's not a feeling, that's a thought. What do you feel?" "I feel I may fail it." And so on. This particular person is feeling apprehensive, anxious, worried, perhaps a little angry about having to write what is to him a meaningless test. He has not yet learned to identify his feelings because he spends too much time intellectualizing. Another example, on a somewhat different level: "Do you trust me, Ben?" "Yes, I do." Consciously he does trust me. But when I ask him to stand up and let himself fall backwards, assuring him that I will catch him, the feeling he gets in the pit of his stomach as he hesitates is a much truer measure of his trust than his previous verbalizations.

In essence, what I am saying here is that feelings do not lie. Your thoughts can fool you, but you can trust your body. You can whistle a happy tune and you can tell yourself you are not the least anxious, but if you heart is racing and your voice trembles and your hands shake, man, you are anxious. So the group will ask you to get in touch with your feelings and trace them back to their origins.

Often you will find that really deep feelings are either elicited from you or expressed by you most powerfully through nonverbal means. The trust exercise I have just described is a very simple but direct way of moving below the veneer of civilized thought toward the core of your being. The more often you succeed at getting in touch with your real feelings, the easier it will be for you to become sensitive to your own needs and the needs of others.

"Head talk" is characterized by sentences which begin with such phrases as "I think," "I believe," and the like. Or the use of "you" or "one" instead of "I." By saying, "You often hear of people not being helped by psychiatrists" instead of "I often hear . . ." the speaker is not fully standing behind his statement. Rather than talking about his concerns about his lack of progress, the discussion can easily shift to a philosophical dialogue about the merits of various forms of therapy. Similarly, questions should be totally discouraged in a group. For example, "Are most alcoholics orally deprived?" or "Is there such a thing as too much sex?" should be changed to statements and translated into nonjargon English—"I drink a lot and I find I constantly want to put something into my mouth when I am not drinking. Nothing seems to fill me up." Now you can easily see how the group can dig into the latter statements but not into the former.

Also to be avoided are words like "interesting," "fascinating," "curious," and "nice." If someone in the group tells you that you remind him of his three-year-old and you say "that's interesting," you deserve everything you get. "That's interesting" does not tell us what, if any, emotional impact that statement made on you. It really stops any kind of a give-and-take exchange, and that's why it is not advisable to use such terms. Try to be definite instead of wishy-washy intellectual.

Leaders also have ways which support "head talk." Hackneyed phrases like, "Let's share your feelings with the group," or "What I hear you saying is," or the old chestnut, "What are you going to do about it?" encourage talking about feelings instead of experiencing them.

Gut language uses a lot of four-letter Anglo-Saxon words such as shit, piss, and fuck. I think these words are used so abundantly because, firstly, they are socially forbidden words and the user gets a sense of freedom from just saying them out loud, and secondly (and more importantly), because these words carry a high emotional valence. They are words you learned at a very early age and they are meaningful. There is no reason why they should not be used. After all, words, like human bodies, are not dirty in the pornographic sense. So if you join a growth group be prepared to hear this kind of language. If you don't wish, you needn't use it, and if it offends you, say so. Then the group will deal with this the way it would with any other issue.

Because spontaneity is highly prized in groups, people sometimes come out with little gems of their own: "That freezes my tits and burns my ass." Or one of the group members described a person she met the other day as "a spherical asshole" meaning all of this person was "assholish."

Hip terminology has become a very strong influence in group, and you will find I used it liberally in this book too. I like these expressions because they are simple and to the point. Phrases like, "where it's at," "up tight," "far out," "turned on," "turned off," "bad vibes," "a downer," "a bum trip," "rip off," "heavy," "stop hassling me," "hang loose," and "let it all hang out" keep people at a feeling level instead of providing an escape hatch for their heads. There is a vast difference between saying to someone, "You are projecting," and "Don't lay your trip on me." "Laying your trip on me," really expresses the interpersonal and inappropriate aspects of the interaction. "Projection" is a psychoanalytic term.

It takes you back to defense mechanisms which are essentially intellectual constructs, and you need to go through a long,
involved discussion before you can get back to "you and me"
and how we feel about each other and what you are doing
to me and so on.

Once in a while, when people are being authentic, they
say beautiful, poetic things, such as, "I was afraid to reach
out because I bruise easily." When someone feels something
deeply and says it, it touches all of us because it touches our
common humanity. Let us look at an example. The following
poems were written by two different people, neither of whom
were in any way professional writers:

> Mama, mama, I'm sorry
>    you are going blind.
> But maybe you were always blind
>    Blind to me anyway.
> I was blind to me too,
>    Seeing me through your eyes.
> But I am beautiful now
>    I am, I am,
> I am beautiful now,
>    I am doing what I want to do
> —at last,
> I am beautiful now and I'm sorry
>    You are blind to my beauty.

and

> How easy the breath
>    that kills a flame,
> How hard to kindle
>    that light again.
> Cold words kill
>    . . . and
> kind words kindle.

By words withheld,
   a dream may dwindle,
Be careful which dream you clutch
   . . . for dreams come true.

# The Group Ethic

Underlying the kind of behavior and expression of feelings that is encouraged in groups is a natural value system which holds that some things are bad and others good. Freud and his followers have tried hard to convince the world that psychiatrists and other helpers are dispassionate scientist-observers—that psychiatric theory, like mathematics, is value free. Carl Rogers holds that only in a nonjudgmental relationship can a person grow. Ideally, that would probably be true. However, in reality we all bring our prejudices to bear on our everyday life experiences. I'd rather be honest about my hang-ups and be me than pretend to be what I am not.

If you examine closely the ethics of traditional psychological theories, you will find that they all hold a strong male bias and that they value middle-class, middle-American, conservative values. They are authoritarian and use the expert's jargon to discriminate against people or to prejudge their behavior—a psychopath is a bad patient; impulsive acting out is frowned upon as negative behavior, etc. This is quite different from the terms my medical colleagues might use, such as appendicitis or carcinoma, which imply no moral judgment about the patient. (Although, particularly in the past, a diagnosis of V.D. has carried with it strong moral condemnation.)

The kinds of groups that I am discussing have been strongly influenced by the humanistic ethic. Let me list here what I consider its basic tenets:

1) Each person is responsible for what happens to him. While we cannot control all experiences of life, we can choose how we will respond to them.

2) The ideal for relationships between people is one of mutuality best expressed by Buber's "I-Thou" concept.

3) Concerns for the here and now are of primary importance. There is a reduced emphasis on striving, on deferred living, and on competitive attainment.

4) An acceptance of all emotions both negative and positive, rational and irrational as valid parts of one's existence.

5) Man is conceived of as having a capacity for continuous growth and realization of his potential.

Translated into practical group terms, the humanistic ethic means that the group leader will not cajole you into participating if you choose not to and that you are allowed to act in any way you want as long as you don't hurt anyone. Openness, honesty, and directness of communication are highly valued. In other words, don't beat around the bush and don't be afraid to interrupt if what you feel or wish to say seems important to you. If I had to reduce the whole growth-group ethic to only one sentence, I would say, "Participate with feelings and you will grow—sit on the sidelines and observe and you will grow older!"

# Making It in Group

Newcomers to a group usually talk about why they are there and how they want to change—that is, if they talk at all. Beginners feel a lot of stress and usually react in one of two ways. Some people become withdrawn and unobtrusive. In effect they are sending out a little message which says, "I am frightened; let me get used to this place; don't ask me anything; leave me alone!" Others become hyperactive when anxious and will talk without stopping. Some unwary souls may, within fifteen minutes of joining an ongoing group, dispense advice to old members or criticize the proceedings. They usually get put in their place quickly.

After the initial jitters members will talk about the least disturbing things first. They may start with their physical symptoms and their poor life adjustment. Gradually they become more personal. Married people will often go into their job difficulties, then the problems they are having with their spouses, and then, quite a while later, their relations with their siblings and parents. The group really gets going when people begin to react to each other and start making connections between what's happening here and now and what occurred in the past. Relations to other group members, particularly in terms of hostility or sexual attraction, figure high on the list of emotionally charged subjects. Similarly, problems touching on inability to become involved in the group process, fear of change, and readiness to leave the group are topics which emerge frequently.

The following transcript will give you a better understanding of what goes on in a group. I have condensed about a half hour of group interaction into a few pages by leaving out irrelevant remarks, repetitions, and hesitations. Otherwise, this transcript, like all the others in this book, are faithfully reproduced, verbatim reports.

BETH: After last week's session, I was very very angry. I even thought I shouldn't be in this group any longer. I just feel like the claws are at me all the time.

DORA: I was feeling very worked up too.

FRED: I just want to say one thing. That is, last week I felt the strangest tension and I couldn't decide whether it was me and I wanted to leave. Then I thought: This is ridiculous.

BETH: I almost . . . that is why I almost didn't want to come this week. I have got work to do and it is hard, and I don't need any extra tension in my life, specially this hounding that I have been getting for the past weeks.

DORA: Do you have any idea . . . do you realize, why you have been getting all this? I give it to you because I am so irritated with you for not doing anything about your situation.

BETH: I get out and I do as much as I can. [pause] Besides, I don't think that's the real reason for you and everyone else attacking me.

DORA: Well, if you don't believe me you can tell me what you think.

BETH: You're jealous of me.

DORA: Okay that's true, but don't put this into that category, because the reason I've been on you has got nothing to do with jealousy.

BETH: Sometimes I would just like to tell you to go and screw off.

DORA: Well then, why don't you? How about your apartment, have you been able to do anything about that?

BETH: No.

DORA: Are you angry with me for asking you that question?

BETH: No.

DORA: Would you like to have a nice apartment?

BETH: Yes, and I would also like to have a permanent relationship with a man and lots of other things.

THERAPIST: My question is, "When are you finally going to get better?"

BETH: When I stop letting the world control me. When I stop getting scared. When I start trusting myself a little bit more.

THERAPIST: What will you do in order to be that kind of a person?

BETH: Well, last week I deliberately put my movie script down and I rested when I felt like it. I walked outside and decided I was not going to punch myself out for this thing.

DORA: You are scared of losing Tom.

BETH: Not only Tom. I am scared of him [pointing to therapist] thinking that I am a bitchy person. I am not happy. I am not particularly happy with my circumstances but I have to learn how to accept it.

THERAPIST: You are always shifting; it is like going through shifting sands; we can never really get through to the core of Beth, which has kept her going to psychiatrists for the last four or five years.

BETH: If I knew what the core of Beth was, then I wouldn't be here.

THERAPIST: You don't seem to be making the necessary attempt to get to know the core. That is why I and the rest of the group are being hard on you. You're scared, and you always talk about incidentals—your job and money, and illness, and your apartment, etc., etc. That has nothing to do with the core inside that is keeping you an unhappy person.

BETH: To me, the core is a void. I don't know what's in there. [pause] Unless you see someone opening up their guts, you think nothing is happening. [turning to the therapist] I don't know what to say to you.

DORA: I don't think that's what he means at all.

BETH: I wasn't supposed to grow up. I wouldn't be loved if I grew up. I certainly wouldn't be loved if I would be any smarter or better in my work than my brother or my father or my mother. That's why when I get punched up, I just fall apart.

FRED: I'm not punching you up. Not at all.

BETH: I have the feeling that I'm doing a lot of rehashing.

THERAPIST: Yes, you are.

BETH: Well, I'm just answering questions.

THERAPIST: Yes, just being the nice girl and answering questions.

BETH: That's right. I am being a nice girl.

THERAPIST: When are you going to stop being just a nice girl and be yourself?

BETH: I'm afraid people will say, "There goes number-one bitch."

THERAPIST: I would much prefer you being the number-one bitch than the number-one qvetch.

DORA: Is that a Jewish word?

BETH: Yes, it is. It means a person who complains chronically.

ANNETTE: Groups are filled with them.

[general laughter]

BILL: How can we help you now?

BETH: By letting me know that I wouldn't be disliked if I got angry.

SEVERAL PEOPLE: Why don't you try us?

JIM: There is one quality that I like in Beth and she seems to have this more than any other woman in this group, and that is the fact that she often laughs at herself. Isn't that right? Like, when you said qvetch, and suddenly, you know, there was a smile on her face. She kind of lit up.

THERAPIST: That is why I say [turning to Beth] you are just playing at being neurotic.

BETH: That's something else that's upsetting me. Why do I think that I am so neurotic. I feel very funny now. I am embarrassed. [silence] I am wondering how everybody feels.

THERAPIST: Why is there always a need for talking?

BETH: Because I never get anything back. The only time I get anything back is when things are going poorly with me.

THERAPIST: Why don't you rely on your own resources? You have talked; you have thought about yourself; you have looked inward; why can't that be helpful in itself? Why do you need to hear from Henry and Joe and Jean and everybody else?

DORA: You know what Beth? I think you want more and more and more and nothing is quite enough.

JIM: I am really getting hostile with you Beth, because Tom made a statement that you were playing at being neurotic, and whether it's right or wrong, it is a significant phrase and you don't even hear it.

THERAPIST: I think one of the reasons that you were embarrassed a few minutes ago was because you were not playing neurotic. It was a new role and an unfamiliar one.

BETH: Because I was talking all about myself. I think I was embarrassed because I was taught that it's wrong to be alone, to be by yourself, to be on your own.

BORIS: I think you were embarrassed when you were being yourself, because most of the time I don't get Beth. I get a very good actress, but I don't get Beth.

BETH: That terrifies me.

THERAPIST: Well then get terrified. You don't look terrified.

DORA: I think that its terribly hard for you to know when you are yourself and when you are not, but it is certainly something that you need to discover.

THERAPIST: One of the things that I know you do is that you play to audiences all the time and I don't mean you as an actress, but you as Beth who is acting.

DORA: And here is an audience.

THERAPIST: Constantly you think, "How is this going to please them, displease them, what is their reaction going to be?"

JIM: You know, now that you mention about Beth's acting, I took her home after last week's session. I was the only one present and I was just astounded because she behaved as if the room were full of people. I had the feeling that, on some occasions, she was talking to people who were not even in the room. She would go to the door, and she was saying lines through the door and to various parts of the room, probably playing for me, or something. It was like watching a weird performance. She opens the door but she doesn't really open it, she flings it open.

ROSEMARY: Beth, this is not criticism, this is feedback. Not one of us can see ourselves the way we really are. When you are ready to hear him or anybody else who gives you feedback, then perhaps you'll be ready to stop doing things that you yourself don't like doing.

JIM: Even in the group you do a lot of acting, and half of the time I can't hear what you are saying, and often it isn't connected with anything.

BETH: I don't recall making all these scenes and acting like a mad woman.

THERAPIST: If you could only stop, Beth, arguing and just concentrate and understand, just observe your pattern, I think it would really be helpful to you.

BETH: How often do I repeat this with other people? Dora said that I do this. Joe says this. And Jim is saying it.

THERAPIST: And Dan said it when he was in the group. Everybody who has known you has said it at one time or another. You tune out or you get involved with yourself.

DORA: And nobody can break in.

BETH: Yes, and I am wondering why. I am hearing it now, I am recognizing it.

Notice right at the beginning of the discussion the emotional contagion that takes place in groups. If one person gets upset, others will be affected by his emotions. This is desirable because it helps them begin to feel and to question their reactions. The second time Dora speaks, she addresses

Beth directly and confronts her with her own feelings about Beth.

*Confrontation* is a very important part of any growth group. It requires us to challenge the unrealities of the world of another person—a world which, though unreal, feels "solid" to him. Abraham Maslow, in 1967 after spending some time at Daytop Village, suggested that, in therapy in general, mental health workers have looked upon the client as too delicate, too fragile, and so we have been afraid to use this tool. Naturally, we all avoid confrontation because we are afraid of the consequences for ourselves; for he who confronts opens himself to confrontation.

A constructive therapeutic confrontation will usually induce some degree of disorganization. This is necessary for change. It has been my experience that even when a patient has lost contact with reality for a time he can, with the help of a supportive group, reintegrate this experience an hour or two later. He will suffer no more of a side effect than if he had just had a bad nightmare and will be perfectly capable of handling himself in the outside world.

I said "supportive group" because I think the attitude of the group is very important at moments like these. I would not encourage a member to make a really painful self-disclosure in a group which has not been together for a sufficient length of time to develop a good deal of cohesiveness. Otherwise, the person who is becoming aware of some painful areas might be utterly destroyed by another member's panic, look of disgust, or other thoughtless act.

In the above transcript, nine people spoke at various times—a good indication that this is a group-oriented group instead of a therapist-oriented group. The more the group is capable of handling its own problems, the more its members learn to be responsible for their own lives. A group where the leader regularly talks with one or two participants, leaving the others to serve as background or function like the chorus in a Greek tragedy, is not a group at all. That's individual therapy in a group setting and does not make much sense to me.

The beauty of the group approach to personal growth is that you have the chance to get to know eight to twelve people who are going to be honest with you. Some of them will remind you of your mother or father or brother or high school principal and give you an opportunity to finish the unfinished business of the past. The group approach thus affords you the opportunity to experience multiple relations.

With a therapist you can never (or not for a long time anyway) be quite sure whether he really likes you and cares for you. All you know is that he sees you one hour a week and is well remunerated for it. With your fellow group members you have no such doubts. They have nothing to gain from telling you how they feel about you. If eight people tell you that you are a truly likable and attractive woman, you cannot just shrug it off as nonsense.

The transcript also illustrates well the shift that occurs between here-and-now feelings and reflections about one's childhood. One moment Beth says, "I don't know what to say to you," and the next, "I wasn't supposed to grow up, . . ."

When Jim talks of having taken Beth home after last week's session we touch upon another dimension of group work, extra group activities. There are some leaders who strictly forbid group participants from meeting outside the group. There are others who ask their groups to meet weekly without them in addition to the "regular" sessions. Personally, to require group members not to speak with each other outside of group seems to me to violate the fundamental idea of growth groups, namely, that you grow through relating authentically to other people. If I really care about Bill, who had a rough time in group today, surely I should be allowed to call him and find out how he is doing. People will see each other in spite of the "no contact" rule, so the rule itself will only make them feel guilty about their meeting and impel them not to report it to the group. And I think any rule which limits a person's responsibility for his actions is a bad one.

It is my policy to allow my patients to meet with one another as long as they tell the group about any significant events that occur during such meetings. I have found this arrangement to be extremely satisfactory. The group, as in the example quoted, learns new things about its members which it may never have discerned otherwise. Sometimes the group even has a party, and the ramifications of who said what to whom may fill the agenda for the next two sessions. I believe that no matter how informal the group meeting is, it is still essentially an artificial arrangement. I think it is very helpful to see the same people in different environments playing different roles—like host or drunk or college professor. This allows each person to experience the others as three-dimensional people rather than as players in a drama that takes place once a week at their shrink's office.

Speaking of once-a-week office visits: There are many people who look upon their therapy as "the thing that happens between five and seven on Wednesdays." That is a no-no. Therapy, like education, must not be confined to just two hours a week; it must not be isolated from the rest of your life. Rather, therapy must become an integral part of life. Therefore, following each session, you should set aside some time when you can quietly think about what just happened. Take stock of your feelings and reactions. You may wish to keep a journal and write some notes in it about what you would like to bring up in group next week. This journal can also be used on the weekend to jot down any dreams, poems, or thoughts that occurred to you between sessions. If you wish, and if the group does not object, you may also record the session on a tape recorder and then listen to it at home. You will be quite surprised at how much you missed during the session and at the new insights you gain into yourself, especially if you concentrate on such things as the quality of your voice, the pauses, and the laughter.

Following the group meeting, if you feel disturbed by what transpired I strongly suggest that you not drain off these feelings by discussing them with a fellow member, friend, or husband, but rather store them for the next meeting. Using your husband or wife as an emotional lightning rod will not help you get to the bottom of what is troubling you. A good principle to follow is, *Whatever feelings develop in the group belong in the group.*

Before you come to group, try to spend a few minutes by yourself thinking about it: What did you want to bring up from last week? What are you feeling as you think of the meeting? Are you looking forward to it with pleasure or apprehension? Why? Are you making progress? If not, why not?

Some group leaders will suggest you read certain books to facilitate your understanding of the group process. Others will discourage it. I think the choice is really up to you. If you are an intellectualizer and a mental masturbator, it would be best not to read too many books about groups. On the other hand, I think most people can benefit by learning more about some of the key concepts and practices of humanistic psychology, gestalt therapy, transactional analysis, primal therapy, and other related areas. Whatever you read, remember that there is no one person or one school of thought that yet has all the answers. Indeed, beware of the person with extravagant claims.

# Hostility and Carnality

Since anger and sex play such an important part in our development and our everyday lives, it is only natural that these subjects should come up frequently in groups. Sessions in which you can cut the air with a knife because it is so thick with strong feelings are usually the very best ones. These feelings usually refer back to parents, fellow group members, or the leader. Because the group leader is central to what happens in a group, I will discuss feelings that relate to him in a separate chapter and concentrate here on anger and sexuality directed at others.

The following brief exchange illustrates the extreme difficulties people have in experiencing their feelings of anger fully. It is one thing to make sarcastic remarks or to take pot shots at your companions; it is another to allow yourself to feel the rage and the pain underneath. In our example, Joe is angry because several members of the group have remarked that his choice of clothes and his general demeanor are effeminate. In order to help him get in touch with his feelings better I placed a couple of pillows in front of him and sat beside him.

THERAPIST: Why don't you take all that anger and put it right into your fist and begin to beat this pillow? [Therapist demonstrates and begins to pound the pillow.] Just do it, let it all come out. [The Patient begins slowly to pound the pillow; he stops.] Think of the whole group and me and your parents and all the other people who have ever done you wrong. [Patient begins to pound the pillow again.]

JOE: Nothing is coming out.

THERAPIST: Make a sound.

JOE: What do you mean, a sound?

THERAPIST: Any sound—fuck, shit,—whatever comes to

your mind; any sound, any word, just let it come out. [Patient still hesitates. Therapist gets behind the patient and picks up both his hands and starts pounding the pillow with the patient.] Just like that, let it come out.

BONNIE: Think of all the horrible people that you have ever met.

THERAPIST: Come on. Let's go. Let's hear it. Feel. Let it come out.

CLIVE: Don't ball it up. Come on, let's hear it.

SEVERAL PEOPLE: Come on, Joe.

JOE: [keeps pounding] I've been bottling up all along for Christ sake.

THERAPIST: Let's hear it. Let's hear it. Let's hear it. Let's hear it.

JOE: I can't.

CHRIS: Yes you can.

THERAPIST: [his voice rising to the point of screaming] *Hit it. Hit it. Hit it. Let it out. Let it out. Let it out.*

JOE: [suddenly] No I won't, I won't let it out.

THERAPIST: You won't let it out? Why not? [Very calmly now, patient sighs—long pause.]

JOE: Because I'm just so used to hanging on to it, that's all. [His voice is full of resignation.] And I don't know what to do with it when it does come out.

THERAPIST: You don't have to do anything about it. It will look after itself. [Patient lights a cigarette. A long silence ensues which prevails for about two or three minutes. Everybody sits silently and tense, waiting.]

JOE: I'm just so fucking tired of the whole goddamn thing. I'm so sick of it. I guess I should start getting rid of the old stuff, never mind the new stuff. I just thought you such an awful, fucking-stupid group, you have no idea. You're so gross it just absolutely kills me. I have really just wanted to kill them all they were so fucking stupid.

CLIVE:  Who?

JOE: [Patient starts hitting the pillow.] I want to start with my fucking family I guess, and then there was a whole line of just beautiful teachers. You wouldn't believe the bastards I've had. [He keeps beating the pillows.] And a couple of psychologists and a couple of psychiatrists too. [He stops, sighs, long pause—he begins to pound again.] You all take warmth and you twist it into something effeminate, and you take fear, and what you see as fear, you take that and change that into effeminate. You see someone uptight and you take that to be effeminate. It made me so scared when I was a kid that they were really going to kill me.

KIM:  Who?

JOE: I think mostly my father and my brother.

KIM: How were they going to kill you?

JOE: Cut my balls and my penis off I guess. That's the closest I can get to right now. I was really terrified of them.

Did you notice how Joe aborted his feelings of real anger? Sometimes there is a lot of confusion as to what is under our conscious control and what is not. When Joe says, "No I won't, I won't let it out," it is pretty clear to everyone including Joe that if he really wanted to, he could let go. The fear of hurting constantly holds us down. Only by experiencing the pain can we hope to get rid of it.

Many leaders avoid the full mobilization of anger in a participant for fear of what it will do to him and the group. Even if the leaders' anxieties are unexpressed, they will inhibit angry confrontations on the part of the group members. If, on the other hand, the group accepts angry feelings as legitimate and someone does get violently upset, the other members will know how to handle the irate person—to see that he does not hurt himself or anyone else. There are very few patients who flip out completely and become unaware of what they are doing. No matter how deeply involved you are in your fantasy with trying to wrench a belt from your father's hand, a part of you knows where you are and who you are and will look out for your safety.

In order to prevent physical injury, it is a good idea for the group to meet in a room with a thick rug, lots of cushions and mattresses, and as little furniture as possible. Preferably, the walls should be padded too. If you want to have an open, encounter-type of group, you cannot have it sitting in chairs. People who sit act automatically in socially prescribed ways, and the group is not a social gathering. By sprawling out on the floor, a person who gets angry can hit the floor or quickly move to comfort someone who is distressed. I consider chairs, tables, ashtray stands, and the like anathema to meaningful group interactions.

Keep in mind that while some people will readily attack others for various undesirable qualities or slow progress, they are much slower to defend a person who is unjustly attacked or who is in fact making good progress. Unless you offer positive support when you feel it is warranted, two or three members can, with their poorly thought-out comments, destroy a person in group. Often, the negative feelings get more air time in a group than the positive ones, while the latter are just as important and sometimes harder to express.

People with intrapersonal probems who join groups frequently have interpersonal problems as well (or vice versa). In other words, their hang-ups adversely affect their relationships with people in general and those of the opposite sex in particular. Understandably, if they spend enough time in the group, they will start repeating their patterns of relating. By being open about their feelings, group members can examine these ties and identify the neurotic factors at work.

Most group members develop some degree of affection

or loving, sexual feeling for another member of the group. Very few will actually act on it or have an affair—if they do, it usually turns sour sooner or later. Nevertheless, discussing the subject in group, although momentarily embarrassing, is always instructive in the long run. That is why I do not think groups should have a rule against sexual relations (Paul Bindrim, for example, who does nude marathons has such a rule.) The only thing I insist on is that those who have intercourse tell the rest of the group so that we can discuss it as adults instead of snickering about it or condemning it or whatever.

Some of the techniques used in group which involve touching or body contact or massage generally produce a heightened and pleasurable awareness of one's body and only rarely elicit an erotic response. Indeed, participants are often surprised that they are able to experience a member of the opposite sex as a person instead of a sexual object. For many people this is a valuable realization with many positive ramifications. The group, instead of being an opportunity for sexual license (as many people fantasize it to be) is probably more moral than the average church choir. In a group you learn to respect another person for his humanity, and the more you respect yourself and others, the less you wish to exploit them to your own advantage. Moreover, the less neurotic you become, the less you will use sex for relief of tension, and you will not need others to define you as a man or a woman.

## Risking Freedom

The process of change, of growth, of the realization of one's full potential, in spite of all that has been written about it, is still not well understood. We know that a person beomes warped early in life by being deprived of his fundamental emotional needs, or by being overly protected, or by being treated inconsistently. He can also be traumatized psychologically—seeing his mother being strangled by his father—or traumatized physically—having his head immersed in water when he misbehaved. Depending on one's genetic inheritance, environmental factors, and the extent to which one's parents, grandparents, teachers, or friends are neurotic, one reacts differently to life's barrages. Sadly, all of us, having been raised by imperfect parents in a very imperfect world, have been, to a greater or lesser extent, blighted.

During our lifetime we become so used to our defenses that, although we come to realize that we would be better off without them (or at least could exchange some bad defenses which make us neurotic), we hesitate to surrender them. Like J. Alfred Prufrock, we ask, "Do I dare disturb the universe?" Many people are afraid that if they give up their neurotic defenses—which they think make them interesting—they will be nothings. "What if there is really nothing inside me?" is a question I hear at least once a week.

This fear is groundless. When we are able to shed harmful defenses we will discover a more vibrant, sensitive, and interesting self.

How does the group bring about these kinds of changes in its members?

1) It helps you to focus on your problems even if it is only for a limited time.

2) Members, by challenging your way of thinking, feeling, and acting, make you reassess your value systems and life goals.

3) The group provides a climate in which openness, honesty, and self-disclosure are highly prized. By learning to trust others you learn to trust yourself.

4) By being exposed to a whole group of people for a prolonged period of time you learn that not all men are bastards like your father or not all women are masochists like

your mother, and so on. You begin to see people as individuals instead of as stereotypes.

5) The group provides you with a corrective emotional experience. You learn what you have forgotten (repressed)— how to be angry or loving or joyful and how to do so appropriately.

6) You may succeed in going back to your beginnings and in unraveling the mysteries of your past. If you really work hard, and if you are in a supportive group, you may actually relive, in fact experience for the first time fully, feelings you had stopped yourself from having at a very early age. Arthur Janov calls this "having a primal."

7) The group will encourage you to put to the test your newfound strength and wisdom. Until you start making concrete changes in your life, changes that your friends and associates actually comment on, you have not made the grade.

8) And finally, the group will make you leave before you are completely "cured" because the latter will take a long time.

In my opinion, a person is ready to terminate his therapy when he has begun to feel connected and worthwhile and when he believes that he is capable of loving and being loved. Such a person will have lost most of his symptoms and maladaptive patterns of living. He is now on the right track and is self-propelled toward continuing growth. He is now strong enough to strike out on his own.

In the following illustration, a forty-year-old woman who has been in therapy with various doctors for four or five years is beginning to think of terminating therapy:

LORRIE: For the first time I am beginning to feel that these positive changes that other people seem to have remarked on in me are truly happening to me. I am just so awed at the fact that I am not as weak as I always thought I was. There are a number of areas in which I still have to make some advances. Now I am able to concentrate more on listening to other people instead of constantly being absorbed in my own problems. This week I was thinking. I wonder how much longer I will attend therapy? I do know that I need some more time.

THERAPIST: You don't seem to have any more of those mental blackouts that you used to have, you know, when you sort of completely turned off and could not remember what was said to you and could not answer to anyone who was speaking to you at that time, particularly if the subject had anything to do with sex.

LORRIE: Right, that hasn't happened for quite a number of weeks. And today something very positive happened to me outside in the waiting room. I said to Harriet I am going to the doctor tomorrow and he will hypnotize me in order to help me give up smoking, and she really laid into me saying, "You're always going to the doctor," and so on and so forth, and I, to my surprise, didn't feel the beating in my eardrums that I always get when I get scared and I didn't think twice about answering her. I didn't feel all crippled inside the way I used to. She didn't leave me all shook up. I felt so elated.

GERALD: You were pretty angry though, weren't you?

LORRIE: Yes I was. If I was angry I am glad. It was appropriate for me to feel this way.

GERALD: I also remember in the past, whenever you got very upset, you used to hold onto your throat and just scratch yourself all over your chest and arms. You don't seem to do that anymore.

MARGE: I think Lorrie has improved tremendously, especially during the last few weeks.

Often the threat of forcing a person out of a group (usually as a result of his poor participation and lack of effort at self-exploration) will mobilize his anxieties to the point where he really begins to get down to the nitty-gritty. The following example illustrates this point. It is a letter written by a group participant following a tumultuous session in which she was told to "shit or get off the pot."

Dear Tom:

Everytime my group has asked (begged)—"Barbara, let us know you," I shook my head, I couldn't understand.

Tonight, after group and a long talk with Sazzy, I started to drive home alone and think. The truth hit me pretty hard and I couldn't push away the primitive realization that I am afraid of each and every one of you—and not only the people in the group, but practically everyone I've encountered in the world. That is why I couldn't say how I felt about Alex or any individual for that matter—because most of the time, when I'm on the spot, no one is really an individual to me. They are bodies—arms, legs, heads—people in plural who are going to hurt me in some way. People are either going to push me away or swallow me up—as I've said before. In the long run, I always feel I'm going to get zonked. Therefore, both the passive and the aggressive people frighten me and I've done a good job of warding most of the population off. I've always thought that most people try extra hard to make people like them and they flop 'cause they tried too hard. I haven't even been doing that. I go into my "song and dance" routine to appease people—I'm sort of saying—"There, I've entertained you, I've contributed to your life - now *don't hurt* me - please just leave me alone and don't hurt me." Or rather—"it's all right if you ignore me, as long as you don't hurt me." Pretty sick—one would think I was born in a jungle.

It hurts to admit this, but I know I've felt this way and that mental block had to get pushed away. I guess the impact of almost being ostracized from group forced me to push that block. Ever since I was a kid I felt like I was on the outside of a ring of people. I don't know if they thought I was in the ring or part of it, but I always felt on the outside dying to come in on one hand and fighting it, on the other. My protection, my mask, my defense mechanism is my set-up and also my downfall, (flop— failure—ZONK, whatever) cause in the long run, I call attention to myself and people come a'looking and ZONK!!!—the people who see either push me away, or push me around. What kind of crappy defense mechanism is that. It's broken! And in that case one gets a new one or does without. I want to do without a mask so badly. I don't really want to be ignored by people 'cause if I did I'd be smart enough to keep my mouth shut at all times and keep to myself. I do quite the opposite. Yes, I'm pretty good at getting into other people almost as good as I am at keeping people from getting into me. I am talented at giving gifts, advice, and orgasms to other people, but as I was told, I can't give a piece of my real self. Selfish? No—Scared.

I may be strong enough to make decisions and get along in life alone. I need group—to learn how to form, join and enjoy real relationships. I ashamedly, yet honestly say, I've never felt relaxed with a friend or group of friends in my whole life. It has taken me well over a year (of subconscious vacillation) to be able to admit to myself, "Aggressive me is afraid of everyone." I don't intend to tell the world, but I will tell my group. That, in itself, is frightening—a real put-down, 'though temporary, I hope.

Very sincerely,

Barbara

P.S. Thank God for this letter, Tom, as I nearly phoned you in a flood of tears.

I think Barbara's letter summarizes in some ways everything I have been trying to say here. The identification of her catastrophic expectations—"People are either going to push me away or swallow me up"—her "song and dance" routine to appease people, and the realization, "I want to do without a mask so badly," are all necessary ingredients in her moving from a position of reacting to her environment in programmed ways to having conscious options as to how to act and a greater awareness of who she is.

The next transcript depicts a session where Hank, a 45-year-old civil servant, gets drummed out of the group. Hank is a mild-mannered man, married with two children. The rest you will hear from the group:

BETTY: For my sake and for yours I really feel that you're not giving me anything, and I have nothing to give you, Hank. I don't know how everybody else feels here.

DAVID: You seem quite agitated about him.

BETTY: I'm not really agitated about him, I just feel that I'm in group and I'm beginning to dig my heels in and it bothers me in a way I suppose to have someone who is sitting there and is not giving and not taking.

THERAPIST: So you feel, Betty, that he is letting you down in a sense.

BETTY: Yes, and equally important I have nothing to give to him, because he is not accepting anything.

HANK: Some of your feeling then is based on your opinion that I'm not doing anything.

BETTY: That's right.

HANK: That I'm not doing something to help myself.

DAVID: If you helped yourself more, you would help us.

BETTY: You see, if I could see any change in you, and I haven't seen any in the eight months that I've been here, it is disheartening for me.

DAVID: You are almost a mute testament to your own failure.

HANK: You haven't seen the changes right in this room?

BETTY: That's right, it's the only place I ever see you and I haven't seen any changes.

HANK: Do you see changes in anybody else?

BETTY: Yes, I see quite a number of changes in a number of people here.

JENNIE: It's also a matter of feeling, ah, it's difficult to put one's finger on it, but . . . but a feeling that something is happening . . . that something is going on.

HANK: Well I haven't mixed with the group . . . that's ah certainly . . .

BETTY: No, no that has nothing to do with it.

HANK: Well I have done things outside the group.

MARLENE: [somewhat enraged] But you never talk about them.

BETTY: We are the last ones to know about it.

HANK: [turns to Betty] Have you told us all that you have done?

BETTY: Well you've got to be kidding.

HANK: Well you have told us all your troubles.

JENNIE: If that's what group is about we can send each other a round-robin letter each week. The thing about you is that you never tell us anything, so that when you have actually gone out and done something like the debating club this is certainly something that we would be very happy to hear about. This would have been an indication to us that you were actually doing something.

BETTY: And I'll tell you something else, that it's very, very selfish of you not to have shared this experience with us, because it just may be that you have gone out and done it because of the kind of help that you have received here, and yet you will not even consider giving us any credit for it, or making us feel that we have been part of that success.

THERAPIST: Or perhaps he doesn't think that we have contributed. In which case though, again you should talk about it.

HANK: I was going to bring it up, I just didn't have the opportunity.

[general consternation in the group. "Oh shit"]

Well there are other things that I suppose I could mention.

THERAPIST: That's not the point. The point is that you haven't so far, and if you haven't, then what about Betty's point of your continuing in the group. How do you feel about that?

HANK: Well I don't think that's any reason for not staying in the group.

BETTY: It's indicative of a whole attitude.

JENNIE: We are just using this as an example.

HANK: Well this is one of my hang-ups. O.K., this is why I'm in group.

BETTY: The only thing that will lessen my irritation with you, because that's what I'm feeling, is if Tom will tell me that it's not unusual for someone to be in group for thirteen months and for an individual such as yourself to make no progress. If Tom can tell me that, fine, and if he can't tell me that, then I think you've got to seriously consider your position here and to either get out or start giving something so that I can give you something.

HANK: You mean I haven't contributed anything at all?

BETTY: Well the odd question . . . but even now I'm very irritated with you because you just sit there and you are not reacting.

HANK: I'm reacting.

BETTY: You're questioning me, like an inquisitor for Christ sake.

HANK: I'm trying to find out why you think the way you do.

JENNIE: But she told you that in the first two minutes.

DAVID: You're trying to shift the attention away from yourself to other people again.

HANK: I think I've improved even in this group, even in here I feel that I'm more sensitive to what's going on than when I first came here.

DAVID: That may be, but it's not known to us.

BETTY: For me it's really difficult to come to this group. I don't particularly like coming, and that's why I make sure that I show up to every meeting. But you, you crap out as often as possible, and for very shabby reasons you don't show up.

HANK: Well it turned out that I had the opportunity to take my wife to a show.

OTHER GROUP MEMBERS: You mean you couldn't have taken her out on any other night?

HANK: Well yes, I guess I could have come. Well other people have missed groups occasionally.

THERAPIST: But not for the sake of going to a show.

MARLENE: I think that Hank has never considered the group seriously. I think it's a social thing for him, and he thinks that he's doing something really daring by coming here. He also came in believing that none of us had really any problems, and here we are today, screaming and getting aggravated about things that have been going on for a whole year and I refuse to waste any more time on him.

THERAPIST: Well that's why Betty says that he should get out.

MARLENE: Well that's my feeling too.

JENNIE: Perhaps my reactions are somewhat intensified by the fact that you [turning to the therapist] gave me a gentle nudge a few weeks ago, suggesting that if I didn't get off my ass I would be out the door. I think I needed it, but it also makes me bloody mad that in all the time I've been here you [turning again to the therapist] have not said anything like that to Hank.

BETTY: Excuse me, but Tom did say at the same time that he laid into you that Hank should also get off the pot, but you make an effort and Hank does not.

JENNIE: That's true, I heard it then, but the point is how long has Hank been here before that?

THERAPIST: Well you know, I was willing to make some allowances for the fact that he's older and more staid in his ways, and that it will take him a longer time to get moving, but now I feel that you've had enough time and that you're not trying hard enough to contribute. It can no longer be said now that it's a matter of you not knowing the ropes. In response to Betty's question I think that for some people it does take twelve months, but personally I don't have the temperament to take any longer this kind of mini unfolding. My satisfaction comes from seeing people move, and when it takes that long a time, I start losing interest in them and I too find myself giving less than I give to a person who I see making progress. So that even from my own personal standpoint I'm getting dissatisfied with your staying in the group.

HANK: Well I brought this up, and I agree that in some ways I'm actually worse than when I came into the group.

BETTY: That would be fine if you were worse, but you're not worse, you haven't changed one bit.

HANK: In some other areas I can see progress.

SANDY: But you don't tell us about it.

HANK: I feel that the group is stirring things up in me. It has precipitated a lot of things that are lying or were lying dormant and this has caused some of my discomfort.

BETTY: Well then why are you suggesting that you should leave then?

HANK: Because I feel that I now need time to regain my balance.

MARLENE: In other words anything that you feel you have gained, you want to repress or sublimate. You just want to push it back and forget all about it.

BETTY: I know I'm going to feel like a real shit when this is all over, but that's something else. We shall discuss that some other time. What you are saying to me it seems, is that you are coming to group and finally something is happening to you; so you want to leave because this something is happening to you which you wanted to have happened to you all the time.

JENNIE: Good God, you had your balance before you came in here.

HANK: Right.

THERAPIST: Then you, for reasons of your own, which don't happen to coincide with ours, agree that perhaps this might be a good time for you to stop coming to group.

HANK: I figured the end of this month—another four weeks.

BETTY: Why the end of this month?

DAVID: I really think that you are a very, very, frozen kind of person, I feel afraid for you.

HANK: Why?

DAVID: Because what you have built up is so tremendously artificial. I react negatively toward you Hank because you seem to be essentially antilife, because you invite hostility, and because you are passive in your perversity. You really bring out the worst in us, me at least, anyway.
[A number of members agree.]
I'm just completely aghast that you have been so passive all this time.

BETTY: Selfish, selfish more than passive.

DAVID: That's true, and still that passivity. I can't understand because you must have trouble, you must be hurting,

and, at times it must be clear to you that you must make a
greater effort, and yet it's not evident in your behavior.
You also invite evil words because I think of you as just a
tremendously immature, complaisant, grotesquely fat slug
behind a rock with never the effort to move out.

THERAPIST: Well, Francois, has he been helpful to you?

FRANCOIS: No he hasn't, he has given me one book to
read. I feel kind of neutral about him.

[General laughter in the group.]

THERAPIST: You say you feel quite neutral to him.
[to Francois] Does Betty make you feel neutral?

FRANCOIS: No. I have some sympathy for Hank because
I've some of the same problems, I've difficulty expressing
myself the way he has.

ADRIAN: I get a real feeling that this is an unfair thing to
do to one person. I recognize that there's a great danger to
myself, that some of this may happen to me one day, but
I also feel that the decision to exclude Hank from the group
was already made a few months ago when I joined the group.
[general comments to the effect as, How come? How so?]
It was obvious to me when I joined, I mean that nobody
listened. On the other hand, I also feel that whenever someone in the group really starts getting to some depth, Hank
always manages to ask a question which gets us off the topic
and on some irrelevant issues. Sometimes I want to come
and hit you because you have this pedant, boring, pompous
way about you. It's really so annoying, I just feel like screaming at you, "Hank, shut up!"

SEAN: I too feel kind of empty towards Hank.

THERAPIST: I think it's always upsetting to everyone to
be part of an experience such as this where one member is
being asked by the group to leave. I think there's a strong
enough feeling prevailing in the group at the present to
indicate that most people feel that you have gone about

as far as you can. This doesn't mean that six months from now, in another group, or in another way, you might not be able to make progress.

HANK: Well you can't fire me, I'll quit.

DAVID: That's very silly, I don't think it has been decided that you'll leave the group. I think it's now incumbent upon you to get some courage going and to work hard to convince us that you should stay. Our problems are too urgent to be bogged down by you.

HANK: I feel that I've gotten about as much out of group at this time as I can, and I intend to quit at the end of this month.

JENNIE: Why at the end of this month?

HANK: I feel another four weeks may be quite useful.

BETTY: They are not useful to me.

JENNIE: Another four weeks, another eight weeks, another three years might be useful.

BETTY: In what way would four weeks be useful?

HANK: Rather than have a sudden break, I think it's valuable to prepare yourself for it.

JENNIE: What about the rest of the group?

BETTY: What about me?

HANK: I'll tell you what about you. I think I've given you as much, as many comments as anybody in here.

BETTY: I'm not after your fucking comments.

JENNIE: We don't want comments, we want you. We want you to give of yourself.

HANK: Do you feel that everybody else in the group has given more than I have?

BETTY: Yes.

JENNIE: Fight back on something that's important, like I've given this or that to that person, I've given compassion, I have cried when this person was crying. Say something that's important.

DAVID: You haven't been totally worthless, but there's certainly no sense in talking about the scattered few incidents that have been only of superficial help to other people in the group, Hank. Nine people for the past hour were being everything from extremely hard to mildly negative toward you, and yet you wish to stay for another three weeks in a group of that sort. I think that's either insensitive or a lot of guts. I can't make up my mind which it is.

BETTY: Not guts; maybe if you said that "well, because of my experience here today, I'm beginning to see things differently, things are beginning to open up, I'm beginning to understand what I'm all about," then maybe there would be some sense in your staying, but you're not saying anything of the sort.

JENNIE: I can quite appreciate the fact that you want to feel as if you had made the decision, that you are not being booted out. It's not a very pleasant way to feel about oneself, but surely all that has been said for the last hour must have made some kind of an impression on you.

THERAPIST: Like, did nothing that has been said for the last hour make any impact on you?

MARLENE: I think his masochism would keep him here for another three weeks.

DAVID: I think we should impose our will on you.

JENNIE: Either you give us some pretty damn good reasons why you should stay longer or you should get out now.

HANK: How magnanimous all of you are.

BETTY: Jesus, just makes me feel like stringing myself up listening to you. Of course what I'm really saying is that I would like to string you up.

MARLENE: I've been sitting with Hank for more than a year, and I say, "Hank, get out."

ADRIAN: Obviously you want to get out of the group and I see no reason why it shouldn't be now, instead of in three weeks time.

HANK: You are suggesting that this should be my last time?

ADRIAN: Well I'm suggesting that the decision is yours.

THERAPIST: Marlene has very clearly stated that it should be the last time.

ADRIAN: You have stated that you wish to go, and since I don't see how you can benefit us by staying here another three weeks, then I think that you should go now.

THERAPIST: Hank hasn't asked to leave in three weeks, he has stated that he will leave in three weeks in order to phase his therapy out.

HANK: All I'm saying is that I've made a decision to leave at the end of January. All right, the group then feels that this should be my last night.

DAVID: Well I think it's contingent on what you're going to give us tonight.

THERAPIST: Well obviously nothing.

DAVID: Are you going to quit?

HANK: Yes.

DAVID: Even your last minutes here are so self-deceptive, so self-deceiving, so unauthentic.

THERAPIST: Three times I've explained to you the difference between asking the group to leave, and you making up your mind on your own and telling the group that you will leave and you have not reacted at all to this—not reacted at all as if you understood the difference. You just repeated yourself again and again and again.

BETTY: I'm telling you this, if you should continue to come for the next three weeks on the same basis with the same attitudes as you have come in the past, I will put you out bodily. I will not tolerate being in the same room with you.

DAVID: If you're going to quit, then if you have any pride at all, you should get up and leave now.

HANK: What would you suggest that I do, Tom?

THERAPIST: Just listen to what people have said to you. I can tell you what I would do if a group felt this badly about my presence in their midst. I would pick up my belongings and would leave. Sure. [Everybody in the room agrees.] I would go and pitch my tent somewhere else, or I would fight.

SEAN: You are ready to go, so why don't you go?

DAVID: You're right at the wire now so why don't you make up your mind right now?

[long pause]

HANK: Before I pick up the few marbles that I have still got left and leave, I would like to make a suggestion that has nothing to do with what we have been talking about, and that is that I think a lot of people here would find it helpful if each day they would spend a little bit of time just writing down their thoughts, kind of a free association type of writing. I started doing that a week ago and I find it's helping me.

DAVID: I find this profoundly depressing.

HANK: This is the first time that you have had anybody drummed out, isn't it?

THERAPIST: No, no.

BETTY: You have not been drummed out.

THERAPIST: You told us that you were quitting in three weeks.

HANK: Oh, yes.

BETTY: Even now you still have options but you have not chosen to pick them up. You're not going to make me feel guilty.

HANK: Before I leave, I don't want to be too melodramatic, but I would like to say that I appreciate the help that you people have extended to me.

JENNIE: Why don't you just say, "Up yours."

HANK: No no, no I really do, I really do appreciate it. I have enjoyed it. . . . I am a little bit resentful.

THERAPIST: You have been of some help to certain people here. You have gone as far as you want to go. This is not far enough for us. So I think we have to part company.

After a few exchanges of this sort, Hank finally picked up and left. During the last eleven years, I've witnessed only three or four people leaving under similar circumstances. Most of these were pretty well along Hank's line—very passive, unable to interact in the group, unable to ask questions or to give of their feelings. On the other hand, I have never seen another person who was neither willing to fight to stay nor eager to blame the group for his lack of progress, when so blatantly told by the group to leave.

I am not neutral in this matter. The statement, "It can no longer be said now that it's a matter of you not knowing the ropes," indicates to the group pretty clearly where I stand. Hank is a good example of a passive/aggressive personality constantly shifting ground. One moment he says, "You mean you have not noticed all the changes I have been going through?" This makes the other members of the group feel guilty. They may think, Perhaps we are being too hard on this guy. The next moment he says the opposite: "In some ways I'm actually worse than when I came into group." The point of course is that he is playing "No one can help me." If he had improved in some ways, or if he had gotten worse—and a lot of people do get worse before they get better—he should have talked about it in group. If you don't talk about yourself no one can help you. And so once again Hank's life script, like a self-fulfilling prophecy, came true.

You can observe clearly Hank's resistance to change when he says that things have been stirred up in him as a result of group and that he wants now some time away from group to let his feelings settle down. This, of course, is the very opposite of what a person should do who wants to get to his core.

Notice, too, that in spite of the general and pervasive hostility that existed in the group toward Hank he was given plenty of opportunity to reconsider. For instance, David says very clearly to him, "I don't think it has been decided that you'll leave the group. . . . Work hard to convince us that you should stay." The group is very reluctant to throw out a member in whom they have invested a lot of time and effort. Those participants such as Adrian and Francois, who see themselves as similar to Hank, also fear that they might be next in line for the guillotine.

Yet a person who is coming to group without benefiting from it or helping others, even if he is a "nice" quiet person, slows down the progress of the other members. I think an ethical leader needs to point this out to such a person, both to protect the individual and the group. Furthermore, as I have indicated before, confronting a man or a woman under these circumstances is just the added incentive a person may need to overcome his anxieties and graduate from observer status to full-participant status.

I would like to close this chapter with a letter from one of my ex-group members who left of her own accord:

Dear Tom:

I miss group. As I see it now, it was a tremendous privilege to be in group. I think that the experience of group is the most valuable in my life so far because it somehow has created a stability, a basis, by which or on which other experiences can be judged or weighed. I hope you can tell what I mean.

I find it difficult to explain. . . . Anyway, group is a good thing and does people good. I will miss not being part of so many lives. Richard I will miss more than others.

I will miss you. It is a pity that you have to be a shrink

all the time. Not that there is anything wrong with being a shrink but I was thinking it would be nice if you could be a friend after you had been a shrink then you could come out with Maggie and me and have a nice friendly time. Still, that's life. I hope it continues worthwhile for you. Have a super holiday. Thank you for so much.

Love,

Vera

## Summing Up

I have tried in this chapter to address myself to the question of what to do before, at the start, during, and after group in order to gain the most from this experience. I have stressed the importance of a clearly understood initial contract, the special ways of thinking and behaving which are most conducive to change, and the point at which a person is ready to terminate his therapy.

# VI

# The Helpee-Helper
# Alliance

For every "helping" relationship, we can ask what it takes to be a "good" participant-client-patient, what it takes to be an effective facilitator-leader-therapist, and what is an ideal bond between the person seeking help and the person attempting to offer it. Reaching beyond the confines of group work we can examine all situations, whether group or individual, where one person tries to learn something meaningful from another.

In order to simplify matters I shall use the patient-psychiatrist relationship as the prototype of all helping relationships. I am doing this because as a *psychiatrist* I am most familiar with both sides of the patient-psychiatrist dyad; because a person who is willing to identify himself as a psychiatric *patient* is more desperate for help than a student, T-group participant, or encounter group member; and, finally, because psychiatrists are the most highly trained and ideologically conservative members of the helping professions. In dealing with the two extremes on the helpee-help scale—patient and psychiatrist—the reader may position himself along this spectrum wherever he feels he belongs.

# Patient-Desired Qualities in a Therapist

The qualities that patients look for in their therapists can usually be categorized as follows:

1) Expert—Some seek a detached scientist who will have all the answers and either tell patients what to do or manipulate them so cleverly that they will automatically do the right thing. Patients with these fantasies often ask for psychoanalysis, hypnosis, drugs, or behavior therapy.

2) Parent—Some are expecting to find an indulgent parent who will coddle and support them and be very gentle. Others are looking for a punitive parent who will break through their defenses, find out how bad they really are, and punish them for their transgressions.

3) Friend—Some patients want to prove that they are just as bright and successful as the therapist, that they are equal, and that they could be friends.

4) Lover—By trying to involve the therapist sexually some patients hope to feel reassured about their sexuality. Short of sexual relations, men want to learn from a male therapist how to be more masculine, and women, by feeling desired, how to be more feminine.

These categories are not as distinct in people's minds as I have outlined. More often than not patients are looking for a combination of qualities in their therapists.

The fundamental questions of any growth experience are: How much should a person's "wants" in therapy be satisfied? What should be denied him to help him fully experience the frustration of unmet needs? And finally, what should be withheld because it might be detrimental?

## EXPERT

There are two polar opposites in our ranks. On one side is the authoritarian, conservative, "elitist," medical-model therapist. On the other, is the authority-denying, democratic, role-leveling, existentialist-model therapist. Let us refer to the former as a "traditionalist" and to the latter as a "radical humanist."

For a helping relationship to be effective, both the supplicant and the guru must share the same set of values and goals. In other words, if person X conceptualizes his problem as, "I need some pills to make me feel better," and he goes to an organic psychiatrist who believes that pills are the answer to X's problem, he will get what he wants. Each of them will validate the other's life philosophy. The "traditionalists" tend to see people as biochemical systems; they are really engineers at heart. If a wheel squeaks, oil it and all will be well. Many of them are effective, and people who trust authority implicitly and who have no wish to dwell on their unconscious motivations are helped by them. Contrary to the "humanists," "traditionalists" have fewer doubts as to the efficacy of their work. Like their patients they avoid asking too many questions of themselves.

In traditional psychotherapy a person who is willing to assume the status of patient seeks help for what he believes to be a sickness. The psychiatrist obliges him by labeling him as such. Anyone can find some psychopathology in every living soul. For instance:

When a patient is early     — he is anxious!
When he is late             — he is hostile!
When he is on time          — he is obsessive-compulsive!

Because this is such a closed system, it does not allow for growth, and each visit reinforces the patient's feelings of inadequacy as his dependency on the father or mother figure grows. At this point the psychiatrist usually offers an interpretation of the exaggerated dependency needs of the patient.

But mental disease is not like any other disease. Nor should psychiatrists act like other medical specialists. The medical model is one-sided, authoritarian, and based on power politics. It does not serve well the requirements of people seeking psychiatric help. For a psychiatrist to reduce a person to a patient and to continue to relate to him as if he were a six-year-old from Mars is both degrading and destructive. Within such a relationship a person cannot grow at his own speed, in his own way.

The "radical humanist psychiatrist" leads by invitation and by his example of continued growth. Only growing people evoke growth in others: fossilized people produce fossils. Patients, like students, only learn from people they respect, and they turn against those who theorize one way of life and live another.

It is important to keep in mind, before you judge them too harshly, that many of psychiatry's training methods and ideologies interfere with the development of a humanistic ethic in their ranks. Many psychiatrists become embittered, disillusioned, and small-minded through years of struggle, first in medical school and later in establishing a practice. Their feelings of caring and compassion and the idealism which first brought them to the study of medicine often are beaten out of them.

Those of you who would perceive them as apolitical and nonjudgmental should remember that in their daily practice, psychiatrists constantly have to make decisions as to what is moral and good. Whether they tell a person to be more assertive or more open, or to change a job, or even if they don't say anything at all, their presence, their listening attitude, the occasional nod of the head communicate implicitly or explicitly their approval or disapproval. On the other hand, their education, the people they know, and the income they earn give them a certain influence and power in the community. Whether they like it or whether they don't, they are deeply involved in issues of morality and power.

The "radical humanist's" knowledge and skills make him an expert in his field. He blends these with his personality to influence people in growth-producing ways. Because he knows himself, he neither exploits his patients to further his own ego trips nor utilizes his professional expertise to keep people at a distance from him. The humanist psychiatrist is a participant in the group. He joins in the exercises and answers members' personal questions about himself. The leader's willingness to risk himself and to become vulnerable enables the group members to do the same. Only by relinquishing their white coats and diplomas on the wall and acting like ordinary Joes do therapists encourage their patients to drop their own masks.

This process of shedding his hard-earned status and getting off the pedestal of course makes the life of the therapist a lot harder. Suddenly he is answerable to his patients. Sometimes he is found lacking in skills, knowledge, or sensitivity. Once he stops pretending to the world that he is omniscient, he discovers that he is human like the rest of mankind.

## PARENT

Many patients have great difficulty accepting their psychiatrist's fallibility, and when they do, this often marks a turning point in their therapy. The following excerpt from a group therapy session will prove enlightening in this respect:

OSCAR [to Ted]: You seem to want Tom to be straight and honest and brilliant and all things and you don't seem to allow for any kind of human flexibility or frailties. The rest of us can have our faults and screw up, but not him.

TED: Well, I would like him to be perfect, at least so far as these matters are concerned. Yes, that's true.

MARK: I feel like you do, that we want someone out there to be so goddamn strong, that we can test over and over again to see how much hostility and anger we can throw, and how much they can take without going under.

DANNY: I agree with you on that.

MARK: And I get frightened when the person I'm hurling abuse at begins to weaken—what I would call weaken, actually the person is just being a normal human being, but I want a super human being, superdaddy. I feel it here more than I've ever been able to feel it with my father. I'm so mad at him, that he did not live up to advance billing. He led me to believe that he could do everything, he talked that way, there was no problem that he did not have something to say about. . . . You could ask him a question about anything and he would have an answer. The guys I served with in the navy said the same thing about me. It doesn't matter what I ask you, you have an answer.

DANNY: You said two things, one about superdaddy, and the other about your father not living up to some kind of advance billing.

THERAPIST: Your father never said, "I don't know"?

MARK: No, he never said that. I don't think those words ever crossed his lips, so I think some of the fault lies with him too, not just with me. And I continue to act automatically the way he did. The moment anything comes up, I've got an opinion, and I can't even stop myself. There is something deep in me that cries out for a male who is bigger and stronger than I am, and yet who will sit down with me and say, "I don't know."

Oscar really sums it all up when he says to Ted, "You seem to want Tom to be straight and honest and brilliant and all things and you don't seem to allow for any kind of human flexibility or frailty." Mark expresses the age-old wish of the child who needs to be reassured of his parent's love: "We want someone out there to be so goddamn strong, that we can test over and over again to see . . . how much they can take without going under." Those of you who are fathers or sons will, I am sure, reverberate to Mark's last sentence: "There is something deep in me that cries out for a male who is bigger and stronger than I am, and yet who will sit down with me and say, 'I don't know.'"

Children need this same combination of strength, sensitivity, and honesty if they are to grow up whole. If they do not receive it, then no matter what the therapist is—authoritarian or democratic—they will cast him in the role of the parent they had but will hope that he turns out to be the parent they always longed for.

## FRIEND

It is difficult to become friends with psychoanalysts and organic psychiatrists. For example, Slavson, one of the most

eminent analytic group therapists, recently said: "Patients
and therapists who seek pleasure are, in fact, in a state of resistance. Inner change is accompanied by discomfort and
suffering. As Schopenhauer stated: 'Suffering is the crucible
in which the human soul is purified.'" Psychoanalysis, like
all fundamentalist religions, sees man as essentially evil,
constantly fighting the devil and the creator (in psychoanalytic jargon the id and the superego). Consequently, the
psychoanalyst is a stern taskmaster—aloof, unapproachable,
always right. He will not answer any questions of a personal
nature about himself, will not see the patient's relatives, may
not even say hello to the patient if he meets him on the street.

Because every patient who comes into therapy has feelings of low self-esteem and wants to improve his self-image,
he will use his whole repertoire of maneuvers to become
accepted by the therapist as an equal. When these tactics do
not succeed, at least two important things happen. First,
the patient feels rejected. The successive rejections he experiences in an authoritarian form of therapy awaken long-
repressed feelings, and if properly handled, they burst
through the abscess and drain at least some of the pus for-
ever. Thus, the patient will not find a friend but will become
a more integrated human being.

Second, the therapist's emotional detachment forces the
patient to focus on his own internal environment. If he is
unable to work his way gradually to the core, the process
becomes an obsessive itch-and-scratch kind of reflex activity
instead of true therapy and may lead to several years of un-
successful analysis.

In chapter V, I mentioned that the humanist therapist
believes that the ideal relationship between people is one of
mutuality best expressed by Martin Buber's "I-Thou" concept. Patients often strenuously resist relating on this level
to their therapist. For some it takes months to call their

therapist by his first name. Yet the most intensive and thera- peutically crucial feelings are those that directly bear on the patient-therapist relationship. Whether the therapist is angry, bored, or caring does not matter as long as he is ex- perienced as real. The therapist's authenticity allows the patient to shed his defenses and risk being himself. By find- ing out more about the therapist the patient will hopefully learn to know him and respect him.

There are many difficulties with this approach to therapy. How does the therapist remain objective when he is emotionally involved? Where is the dividing line between therapist-friend and just plain friend? These difficulties can be overcome if the individuals concerned are open and honest with each other and seek the help of the group when- ever necessary. In some cases, particularly when a patient and a therapist feel deeply negative or positive about each other, another professional may have to be consulted to help resolve the impasse.

The following transcript is offered as an example of an open, friend to "therapist-friend" interaction:

PERCY: I feel that very rarely do you ever involve your- self personally to the point of giving a personal opinion. When you do I always find it very helpful. What I would like to see you do more is to get involved as a person in the group. I know the fine line you have to walk, I know it's difficult.

LUCY: I have noticed that you seem so much more relaxed now than you used to be, let's say a year ago, and you seem to be enjoying us more as people. Whether that's just because you know us better or whether it is really because you've changed I'm not sure. I find you attractive as a person. I like you, and I appreciate what you and the group have done for me.

FRANCES: I was just thinking of the weekend and the

tremendous control that you seem to have over your own feelings and being able to keep track of everybody else's feelings. Fantastic. I noticed that everybody was anxious to work with you and cooperate with you. I have also noticed that it is easy to pick on you because you don't lash back childishly.

PERCY: A couple of years ago I said that I would very much like to have you as a friend. I still feel that way.

KARL: Well I like you too. Nine months ago I accused you of not giving enough and in these nine months I have seen you change considerably and I have to disagree with Percy; I think you have reached a point where your contributions are at an optimum without becoming dominant and I'm quite happy with your participation. I too have seen you change, becoming more open, I mean helpful-open, not causing-dependence-open, and I thank you too for the weekend, but not just for the weekend. Hell, further than that, for what may come.

STEPHEN: Yeah, I feel much the same way as Karl does. My experience with one other psychiatrist—the difference in approach is really quite astonishing; I mean it's much more relaxed with you. I don't think you could have done any more than you did on the weekend. At the end of the weekend when you read that poem you sounded like a Presbyterian minister.

THERAPIST: You have no idea how much I would have liked to have sounded like a Presbyterian minister in the early 1940s. [general laughter in the group]

STEPHEN: I think that the reason that some people here have remarked on your change is not because you have changed so much, but because they have gotten to know you better.

NANCY: I think you're cute. [general laughter]

THERAPIST: You're a married woman, you've gotta watch it. [general laughter]

NANCY: And I like your humor, I like the spontaneous thing that happens between you and me and between you and other members of the group. I know how much preparation and work goes into what you do, particularly the weekends—and I appreciate it. And I too find you're becoming more relaxed. When you wear your jeans they're creased more often now than they used to be and last weekend one of your pockets was folded down; it wasn't pressed properly the way you usually wear them.

FRANK: I have been to two or three psychiatrists before and the first time I came to the office here I realized that I have only been coasting before. Like right away you put me on the spot by asking, "Why are you here?" It was encouraging for me to have you fire questions at me which were revealing things to me that I have been trying to keep hidden.

RENATA: I was just sitting here thinking of my first visit here. Following that I had to report back to my individual psychiatrist, and I told him that you were the most sarcastic, sardonic person I have ever met in my life.

THERAPIST: If you feel differently now, would you mind having a little chat with your psychiatrist? [general laughter]

RENATA: I should; I will.

THERAPIST: Please do.

RENATA: Really my attitude toward you has changed so tremendously. I think that you really are a very warm, caring kind of a human being. I think you have a beautiful way of telling something to someone that in itself might be devastating, but the way you say it, a person can listen to it without taking offense. You always leave me knowing where I'm going—like what to do with the information. I like you. One thing, though, I really do resent is the way you pass out pills. I believe that people should overcome their problems without pills.

THERAPIST: I think there is much truth to that. I just don't like to have a lot of hassles about pills. Should you or shouldn't you take them—should I give you twenty-five or thirty. Well last month you used thirty, this time you should have twenty-five. It is so easy to get pills today. If I don't give it, the general practitioner or the obstetrician is going to give it. I feel that in the long run I have more control, more knowledge of what's going on if all the pills that a person is taking originate from here instead of all over the city. I agree wholeheartedly that people should not be on pills.

NANCY: Well, I know that in my case I was on a lot of pills when I came to you, and if at the beginning you would not have renewed those prescriptions I would have stopped coming to you. And I also felt very responsible for how many pills I would take and I tried, because of the confidence you expressed in me by giving me the pills, to take as few as possible.

PERCY: That's the way I feel. Tom gave me a prescription about four weeks ago and I haven't even filled it, and if he would have refused to give it to me, I'm sure I would have gotten somebody else to write the prescription and fill it.

THERAPIST: Well, let me pull a few things together. We're talking about growth—growth in other people, growth in me—how people change. As I indicated before, it is not easy to change. There are certain personality characteristics which are going to be with us for a long time. Several people commented on the fact that I was more at ease and that I've changed. I think that's true to a large extent. But it is a two-way process; with some people I can feel uptight and with other people I can let go. So to some extent it reflects on our relationship. Because of the results that I'm getting I also feel a lot more confident today about the kind of therapy that I'm doing than I did a few years ago. So although I don't think that I have changed my therapeutic techniques or my ways of relating to people, I think that I have acquired a certain strength of belief in the rightness of what I'm doing, which permeates my whole being and makes me feel more at ease generally as a therapist and as a person.

Although this does not bear directly on the topic we are discussing, let's pause for a second to look at Renata's perception of me on her first visit. I recall once seeing a girl for a consultation; during her next session she acted surprised when she saw me. She explained that she had left her first appointment with the impression of me as a huge, fat man and she was amazed to find me suddenly a man of normal height and weight. Sometimes a patient may attend group for quite a while without ever truly seeing his therapist.

I have found that children up to about the age of six show a similar inability to discern one person from another. You can test this by showing a five-year-old a picture of yourself in a group and seeing if he can tell you apart from the others. I think the cause of patients' and young children's lack of discrimination is probably the same. Both are overinvolved in themselves and lack the ability to empathize with others.

To further emphasize the difficulty that some people experience in differentiating reality from their own projections, and to introduce our next subject—the therapist as a lover—read the following instructive letter.

### DEAR DR. VERNY—I LOVE YOU!
### or
### THANKS FOR THE TRANSFER, I'M ON THE RIGHT BUS NOW

It happened so simply. I tried one day to recall your features, and couldn't. I was startled to realize that after all those hours with you, when I was wailing my life away, person by person, I had submerged your image completely in my torrents of feelings.

Three sessions in a row I tried to make a point of

pinning down even one of your features—an eye, an ear, your chin. Three times I failed. Even your voice eluded me. You coughed once—and I almost had the timbre, tone, and the pitch. But by the time you had your handkerchief out it had faded away.

Then one day your hands came into focus. Such sensible hands—strong, squarish, robust in color, and tipped with very clean, crosscut nails. They weren't just resting there either. They were positively eloquent as they darted through the papers on your desk making decipherable notations. So readable in fact, no druggist would ever have to make an educated guess about them.

Now I was anxious to get all of you in focus, so taking courage I looked right at you and asked mournfully and wistfully, "won't you talk to me."

You looked solidly back and said very meaningfully, "Why, I have been talking to you right along—I have been communicating."

Oh, dear Dr. Verny—that was the moment I saw you altogether! I saw your articulate eyes, the color of moldering brown leaves on a forest floor, glinting with accents of apricot and gold. Your supple lips looked ready to curl into a smile at the least provocation. Your soft, brown hair was damp-combed and briskly trimmed. The round shape of your face bespoke tenderness, belying boyishness with its shadow of a no-nonsense beard lurking underneath the skin.

At last I had your physical image firmly lassoed in my mind's eye and I was trembling in eagerness to glean any little highlight of what makes you you. My stars, Dr. Verny, you were illusive. You kept on twinkling just out of reach. But I did not despair. With a little dib here, and a little dab there, I intuitively came to know much about you. For instance, you coughed again. This time I not only captured the timbre, tone and pitch—but the divine little accent as well. Attacking dead on, I asked you about it. I appreciated your frank answer that you were a Czechoslovakian Jew, and had dallied in Vienna for a few years because that was where all good psychiatrists came from. With all that warm blood in your veins PLUS the cultural advantage of that dalliance—no other statement was necessary.

Another time you made mention of "my wife"; but you quickly corrected yourself and said "Mrs." Verny. I had a bad moment then—but the sun came out again when I realized that it had just been a Freudian slip of the tongue. The Mrs. Verny you referred to of course was your charming "old world" mother. She must stand tall when she thinks of her son "the doctor."

Then there was the night I had the late appointment. I asked you why you worked so hard and you said you would go crazy if you didn't. Dr. Verny, I think that was a great statement for a psychiatrist to make. I knew just how you felt. We really understood each other.

But alas, the end was to come as simply as the beginning. "Why don't you get rid of that parson's daughter hair-do?" you asked, "it's 1967 you know."

Everything seemed to happen at once after that. I got a real devilish new hair-do—and I discovered you had two sons. This bit of news called for some devilish fast rearrangement of the hard learned facts I had of you.

If the boys are four years or under, then the enchantment of marriage and the wonder of fatherhood is still with you. On the other hand, if they are between the ages of 12 and 4 then there is hope. That statement you made about hard work keeping you from going crazy really meant that your homelife was terribly unhappy, and your sons were determined to keep it that way. But then, of course, if they are approaching age 13, they are preparing for their Bar-Mitzvah, as they are getting close to this momentous occasion they need a father—especially a hardworking one.

Dear Dr. Verny, I love you, but two chances out of three those boys are either four years old or 13 years old, and that points me in only one direction. The only place

I'm going with my new flipped hair-do is out of your office. The session is over—but thank you for holding open the door.

Lee-Ann

## LOVER

The number of sexual involvements between patients and their psychotherapists is, according to the findings of Masters and Johnson, quite large. The recently published book by New York psychiatrist Martin Shepard, *The Love Treatment* is, as far as I know, the only book dealing with this subject. Shepard found that six of eleven patients interviewed were actually helped by sleeping with their therapists; three were harmed; and two remained unaffected. With humanistic therapists, the degree of friendliness and affection that develops between patients and therapists can provide a fertile soil, so to speak, for intimacy to develop.

Personally, I do not feel that sexual relations between patients and therapists are a good thing. It is very important for a patient to know that he or she is not being exploited. But the patient-therapist attraction need not be a once-in-a-lifetime meeting of the souls. This is not what the patient stipulated he or she wanted from therapy; it is not part of the contract. In my opinion, the therapist should remind the patient—if necessary—that he or she is in therapy to gain freedom, not a lover.

Dr. Shepard, on the other hand, suggests that the therapist's ultimate responsibility is to help his patient grow and learn, and any and all means should be valid in reaching this goal.

The last transcript in this section illustrates how many of these different role expectations mesh with each other. A good, typical group session will, every once in a while, go off course and then require midcourse correction to stay on its trajectory:

THERAPIST: You were pretty angry last week.

FRAN: Yes, I was; I was very angry. I'd got myself all worked up in a kind of a knot—it was really a ghastly feeling—well, I suppose we'll have to fill Ron and Sally in on what happened. The thing that worried me very greatly was Dr. Verny's sort of allying himself with Joyce. And I'd like you, before anyone else comments—would you fill us in on that—as you remember it. And explain it.

THERAPIST: Why don't you tell it the way you remember it?

FRAN: All right, but I want an explanation from *you*, you see, this is the thing. So—I don't know quite what the opening comment was, but—Dr. Verny said that he dreamed about Joyce and told us about the dream—the part we were told was relatively innocuous, but—I thought it was a mistake on Dr. Verny's part because of the father image in the group. I would have thought it was, from a lay point of view, anyway—one of the duties of a therapist to remain completely apart from any particular member of the group; and I thought that he allied himself with Joyce, set Joyce apart, in this particular situation. He aggravated that by then saying Joyce thought the way he did. This may be very true, very fine, but that, I felt, was a stupid thing to say, frankly. If he thought it he could have kept his thoughts to himself. Now I would like Dr. Verny to explain what his method was to allay my fears in this regard because I thought what he did was quite disturbing.

THERAPIST: Well, I don't think I want to do that right now. I know my feelings. I would like to know what some of the other participants feel, or even the people who weren't here.

ARNOLD: Well, I suppose I had some of Fran's reactions

in the mildest possible fashion. Sitting on the floor seemed silly to me. The thing about Joyce and the dream and the remark about thinking like Joyce. . . . I don't know. . . .

THERAPIST: As you recall, in the dream, I had children at a camp, where I was organizing some very complex war games. Joyce was there too; she was the one that I remembered of the people who were present. Gino thought that I looked upon the group as children, and I was organizing them—getting people to react to each other . . .

FRAN: With Joyce's assistance.

THERAPIST: With Joyce's assistance, almost in the position of a cotherapist, or something like that.

ARNOLD: Joyce had gone to the head of the class. You were pleased with . . .

THERAPIST: With her progress. Yes, because the previous week she had brought a record that I thought was very appropriate.

ARNOLD: It's still a bit of a mystery to me. I still don't see the favoritism. I've certainly noticed at odd times Joyce has made vaguely flip remarks, which I think most of us have. But I can't see the favoritism.

SALLY: I have noticed it—whenever I'm sitting here. I have thought—but I'm paranoid, it's always, "We'll ask Joyce," but . . .

MARION: Hara and I were continuing to talk about manner of dress and reason for sitting on the floor and things like that, going home in the car. I think I felt . . . she was sitting so close to Dr. Verny. They seemed so chummy. I don't know if I want the attention—if I want him to be like that toward me and not toward somebody . . . towards Joyce or the other women . . . I don't know.

FRAN: Well, I asked Joyce where she usually sat and she sat *there*. But anytime that I have seen her—I've been away and she may well have been sitting there for the last six or seven weeks and that's fine—but up to then anytime I have seen her sit on the floor—there may have been one or two exceptions—she was sitting at Dr. Verny's feet. And this I thought was nauseating, to say the least. You were sitting over there. You just managed to sit and look adoringly up at him periodically.

ARNOLD: You're sure about all this, are you?

FRAN: Positive.

BEN: As you made the statement, Fran, I was trying to think back and it still hasn't really clicked in; on-occasion-yes but on-occasion-no kind of thing. So it hasn't registered in that direction with me.

FRAN: It hadn't bothered me until last week, but then everything fell into place.

ARNOLD: It's just hard to get worked up about.

RON: Yeah, again, I mean, fair enough, God bless America. I hadn't particularly thought that the doctor was making a teacher's pet of Joyce.

THERAPIST: I wonder what this discussion will do to Joyce. Because if from now on she feels that what she wants to say in any way agrees with something I have said, am saying, or will ever say, she will be labeled as a teacher's pet. And then, of course, there's the problem of the ultimatum which I was given, you know, "explain yourself or I'll have your head."

FRAN: Not that, no. I said to you that unless there was some valid explanation, I would leave the group. Because to me the problem was that serious.

ARNOLD: Do you still see it that way?

FRAN: I'm prepared to say 98 percent of it is my hang-up, but there is still that 2 percent to be settled.

ARNOLD: Wouldn't you rather settle the 98 percent?

FRAN: I cannot work on the 98 percent until the 2 percent is settled.

THERAPIST: How do you figure that out?

FRAN: Because it is inhibiting.

THERAPIST: It will be even more inhibiting if you leave the group.

FRAN: I haven't had any sort of explanation at all.

SALLY: I resent these things that Dr. Verny—or that I feel—that he does, but I don't think that it should be inhibiting.

FRAN: There's another interpretation, too, Sally. I may well be looking for a way out. And I've faced that too this week. Perhaps this is just what I've been looking for. This is my way out.

THERAPIST: You want to be rejected.

FRAN: That's right.

THERAPIST: With righteous indignation.

FRAN: Right, I've faced all this. I know this is so.

THERAPIST: What is it that's getting to you that you don't like? My feeling is that something must be making you anxious, so that you want out.

FRAN: Yes.

THERAPIST: Now, do you have any clues as to what that might be?

FRAN: I think it is the age-old problem that is really one of the reasons I'm here. That is, to find out why it is that I want people to reject me, because I push them right against the wire, and then I can say, "There you are, you see, I was right, they are rejecting." But I put them in an insupportable position; they have to reject me.

JOYCE: What was your father like? I don't think you've told us anything about him?

FRAN: He was a perfectionist. He was a very impatient man, but not an unkind man, he was a very kind man. When my mother died, I was very conscious of a feeling that I would rather it had been my father who had died, instead of my mother. And yet my mother was very sickly and always a problem. Maybe I was more emotionally involved with her than I was willing to admit, and this was the way it came out—that I would have preferred my father to have died. He seemed to have a sort of laissez-faire attitude. Anything for a quiet life: we have a very sick person here, and let's keep things on an even keel. I know I resented my mother being sick all the time.

THERAPIST: Well, you certainly develop some pretty strong feelings towards men who don't pay enough attention to you.

FRAN: And also, I set impossible standards for men.

ARNOLD: Well, if your father was a perfectionist you couldn't possibly . . . I mean, by definition of a perfectionist, nobody can live up to his expectations.

FRAN: And yet I wasn't conscious of his expecting a great deal of me. I lost a lot of faith in you last week. And this has been coming, this was just, shall we say, accelerated to some degree. I think I haven't been 100 percent convinced. Maybe I want my faith restored.

SALLY: Do you think it is that important?

FRAN: It seems to be. It bothered me enough that . . .

THERAPIST: Well, I'll tell you, Fran. I had this dream, and I thought that it is very rare that I dream about my patients; and I thought this is the first time I dreamt about this group. I always ask them to be honest with me; I can be no less with them. I will tell them about it if the opportunity arises. It was a question of either enduring some discomfort and eliciting some criticism or holding back and being dishonest. And I decided to be open and let the chips fall where they may. It was as simple as that. It was neither a technique, nor do I think it was really a mistake. I just followed the ground rules of the group.

FRAN: Well, I'm quite prepared to accept that. I mean, that's fair enough. O.K.

THERAPIST: I think I could pursue it further where it becomes a little more uncomfortable. I could ask, as you have, why was it that I dreamt about Joyce instead of someone else. I have asked myself that and the answer I come up with is the same as I mentioned last time—that she impresses me as a person who has an easy access to her feelings, which I like. But it doesn't mean that I don't like somebody else for some other quality. It just means that this particular quality appeals to me. About you, another quality—like your logical thinking, for instance, appeals to me. But it is not as likely to be dreamed about because one dreams more about emotions than logic. I might dream about Sally because of her good looks. And I might dream about Ron because of his pirate-like beard. What I'm trying to say is that the dream doesn't mean that I care more about her than about anybody else in the group.

FRAN: It is very good that we can discuss this into the open here. It wouldn't come out in a social group. And from that point of view . . . now, I would have been less than honest if I hadn't confronted you, Dr. Verny, with what I honestly—personalities aside—it was such a tremendous problem in my mind that I certainly couldn't have carried on unless it had been in the open. And .it has sparked reaction. I think sometimes we have great difficulty making this something more than a social group. I think there are times when we look at it as a social group, and then all of a sudden we think—whoops! it isn't. We are here for something far more important than the repartee type of thing. That's when it hurts sometimes. Because you feel "So-and-so is not a friend of mine to say something like that," or "Why am I so outspoken?" But really they are not friends, they are there as people to react to, and to react to you. I think it is awfully hard to divorce yourself from the social-gathering bit.

You will have noticed that Fran speaks first of me as a

"father image" and, in the next sentence, of her expectations that the therapist will "remain completely apart from any particular member of the group." For the rest of the group I should be catalyst, an inert substance serving a specific function, but to her I should be a loving father. Her further reactions, and those of Sally, in particular, indicate that at some level of consciousness her feelings are rather sexualized. For example, she points out how Joyce's sitting at my feet was "nauseating."

This woman, like so many others who have unresolved love-hate relationships with their fathers, is looking for the great "penis in the sky." Just as some men are looking for the biggest breasts they can find—I am speaking here both symbolically and literally—some women spend all their lives searching for a penis that is equal to the one they wanted and never got. The unresolved emptiness within forces them into a pattern of seductiveness followed by anger and rejection. This is another reason why a therapist should never become sexually intimate with a patient. No matter how good he is in bed, he will not be good enough, and there will be hell to pay. Furthermore, since most therapists know this, the chances are quite high that they will be lousy. Thus, sexual relations between patients and therapists usually cannot help either of them.

# The Perfect Patient

The patient every therapist dreams about possesses all the virtues of the therapist—plus some. In addition to the qualities that I have already mentioned, such as attractiveness, brightness, and openness, he should be sincerely motivated to work on his problem. He should trust his therapist with his feelings but never unquestioningly accept as gospel what the therapist says or does.

The ideal patient will talk about his critical feelings toward the therapist in group instead of outside the group. Sometimes a completely innocent remark made by patient X may be picked up by Y, distorted a little and transmitted in its new form to Z, who proceeds to embellish it and passes it on to A, and so on. Before you know it, the therapist may hear from one of his colleagues that one of his patients heard . . . It is the old "broken telephone" routine to which a therapist is very vulnerable.

The task of a psychotherapist can sometimes be very frustrating. He may see a patient for months without any visible changes. At other times a patient who was doing well may lose his job, suffer a sudden relapse, and require additional therapy. It is, therefore, very important for the psychiatrist who cares about his work to know that his patients are doing well. So the perfect patient improves and keeps improving and lets his psychiatrist know once in a while what he is doing (even after he has terminated therapy).

# Summing Up

What the patient says—and even thinks—he wants, namely, to get rid of his symptoms or self-defeating life patterns, is not at all what he really wants unconsciously. What he is impelled to do unconsciously is heal the wounds he received as a small child, which were the result of not having had his fundamental needs met. Therefore he wants his therapist to be a magician, parent, or lover.

The therapist, in turn, is willing to encounter the patient openly and honestly on any level as long as he feels the patient is genuinely trying to make progress. The more the patient is like the therapist, the more the latter can respond to his patient's problems. He can then act like a guide who has been through this dangerous land before and knows the way.

# An Overview VII
## of Verbal
## and Nonverbal
## Group Techniques

Until recently, little use had been made in groups, or in individual therapy, of special techniques or exercises—what are referred to by their detractors as "games" and, in psychiatric language, as "structured interventions." One of the major reasons that nonverbal techniques were frowned upon was the belief—enshrined in orthodox psychoanalytic theory—that "acting out" serves to maintain repression. Therefore, any time a patient attempted to do anything in the therapeutic situation that was other than verbal—whether this was pacing the floor or doodling or whatever—he got his knuckles rapped.

During the last twenty years new psychiatric approaches have broken with tradition on this question. Many therapists now hold that "acting out," rather than aiding repressions, allows a person to see the depth of his real feelings and connect them with his past. Frequently, it is believed, he will "know" the truth about himself without interpretations.

# Pros

What are the advantages of these new techniques? They cut down on the amount of chitchat that goes on in a group, particularly when a new group is just starting. Instead of allowing group members formally to tell each other their names and occupations, a direct instruction, such as "Make a motion and then say your name," will immediately encourage people to interact in more meaningful ways. The use of a technique "unfreezes" people; because of its novelty, an exercise is often approached like a game that promises to be fun. And individuals are much more eager to participate if there is a sense of discovery in what they are doing.

Encounter techniques also bring the leader and the participants closer together. They experience each other in new ways and reveal new facets of their personalities. As you well know, what people say and how they really feel are often quite different—not because they are lying, but because they are living a neurotic illusion. Only when a person is actually experiencing something can he know for certain that it is real. For example, it is very easy to say, "I want to be more a part of this group." It is quite another matter for this person to try to break into a circle the group has formed to test the strength of his desire to be part of the group. Other techniques may involve the formation of various subgroupings, such as dyads, triads, and males versus females. The effect of these exercises is to bring people together in the group who do not interact well with each other. Thus if the therapist says, "Choose the person in the group you have the most difficulty communicating with," he encourages a frank exchange that is probably long overdue.

One of the difficulties of working in a therapeutic way is that people very carefully screen the material they bring up for discussion. Only when emotions run high is there a tendency toward spontaneous expression. By quickly raising the emotional thermostat of the group, the members will reach a dreamlike state of consciousness which will help break down their defenses. The dismantling of the defensive armor is also aided by placing a greater stress on nonverbal communication. For instance, if the therapist asks a verbally facile man to take some clay and mold it to represent his feelings of the moment, the man may, deprived of his intellectualizations, begin to get in touch with his feelings.

Since groups, even those that utilize nonverbal techniques, are still primarily speech-oriented, the members who are not adept at expressing themselves verbally are often at a disadvantage. Nonverbal techniques, such as dance or painting or role playing, give these participants a chance to shine and provide the rest of the group with an opportunity to reassess their ways of judging other people and ultimately themselves.

When one member converts his feelings into actions, not only do his feelings become more tangible, but they have, to borrow a phrase from billiards, a carom effect on the other members of the group. Genuine feelings always elicit a widespread response; as a result, there is a steadily spiraling emotionality in the group, which is exactly what we are striving for. It is at such moments that we experience emotional insight or, as it is referred to in the East, satori.

Of course one insight, even a major one, does not change a person's life. But it does provide a reference point for the future. It gives an individual the experience, no matter how brief, of knowing something about himself with absolute clarity. In a few days he may not even remember what the insight was, but he will remember having it from the feeling of joy it occasioned. This will make it easier for him to reach another satori in the future.

# Cons

Because encounter techniques are simple to apply and easy to learn, many people who aspire to be gurus—although lacking in understanding and training—pick them up and use them on their unsuspecting flock. This fact and over-exposure by the mass media are the main reasons for the public's growing scepticism about encounter groups. The dilettante leader may use a technique when things are dull instead of finding out the reason for the group's lack of zip. Unfortunately the technique may snuff out some very important feelings which, given sufficient time, might have surfaced.

Another shortcoming I have noticed in leaders who become preoccupied with techniques is their staccato approach. Every hour on the hour a new exercise is introduced. Not only is such a leader insensitive to the needs of his group, but by triggering feelings and not providing enough time to deal with them, he is literally creating a time bomb without defusing it. This time bomb is likely to go off when the leader is gone and there is no one around to pick up the pieces.

To these difficulties, others can be added. There are group leaders who get a thrill from turning people on and producing a great dramatic performance worthy of Stratford. In my opinion, creating drama for the sake of drama is indefensible in a group. Also, by using too many techniques, the group will tend to become dependent on them. Members will expect the leader to provide them with entertainment and, like the overindulged, overprotected child, will not be able to function without direction. Finally, in each group there are always one or two individuals who will say, "I hate those games" or "Not another one!" These characters make it difficult for the leader to use a technique, but they are also the very people who, if they can get involved in the exercise, often benefit the most from it.

# The Classification

Encounter techniques can be divided into three categories:

A. TECHNIQUES RELATED TO THERAPEUTIC SYSTEMS (largely identified with a particular systematized therapeutic approach):

1) Psychodrama
2) Gestalt therapy
3) Transactional analysis
4) Bioenergetic analysis
5) Primal therapy

B. INTROSPECTIVE TECHNIQUES (inner directed and performed individually within the group setting):

1) Fantasy
2) Visual and acoustic exercises
3) Art expression
4) Sensory awareness
5) Relaxation and meditation
6) Self-assessment and feedback

C. INTERACTIONAL TECHNIQUES (contact with others):

1) Confrontation exercises (in trust, intimacy, risk taking)
2) Role playing
3) Physical-contact games
4) Massage

# A. TECHNIQUES RELATED TO THERAPEUTIC SYSTEMS

## Psychodrama

Almost all forms of growth groups and therapy groups utilize the techniques of psychodrama. These involve reenacting past or imaginary situations, providing an alter ego to another person, directing several people through a dramatic scene, and the like. Members of the audience may spontaneously join the "actors" on stage or may be asked by the director to play a certain role. Psychodrama encompasses not only words, but also movements, gestures, singing, and dancing. In a short time most individuals learn the principles underlying the roles of protagonist, auxiliary ego, and "double" and are able to carry out role-reversal and mirror activities.

## Gestalt Therapy

Gestalt therapy takes the psychodramatic approach one step further. Instead of asking two members of the group to act as your mother and father, the gestalt therapist asks you to play those parts. Thus, you may have a dream in which you are a falcon. Instead of interpreting the dream—as would an analytically oriented therapist—or asking you to "play" the falcon and someone else perhaps to "play" you, the gestalt therapist will suggest that you be the falcon, the sky, and so on. He may say to you, "Write a script for the falcon and have a conversation with it."

Gestalt therapy works on the assumption that we project a part of ourselves into all the things about which we dream or fantasize. The only way to integrate these fragmented parts of ourselves is by fully experiencing them in the here and now. Patients are therefore helped to confront what they have been avoiding and to reown what they have disowned.

In practice, the gestalt therapist watches for splits in attention, awareness, content, expression, and tone of a person's verbalizations. When he discovers an inappropriate quality, such as a small-girlish inflection in a forty-year-old woman's voice, he will focus her attention on this and ask her to get in touch with this "girlish" feeling.

Interventions in gestalt therapy are noninterpretive, thus encouraging the patient to assume responsibility for his therapy and for his life.

I find that the gestalt approach works best when a person is at an impasse—for example, cannot make up his mind whether he should return to college or not—or with dreams or fantasies. Some people get the knack of it very quickly and have no trouble at all becoming another person or object. Others will simply refuse even to try; they will say, "How can I be a chair? I don't know what a chair feels like." These individuals can often benefit by a slow process of gestalt awareness training, where they are asked to imitate another person in the group, then to play their mother, a policeman writing a summons, and so on. Watching others in the group demonstrate the technique is often helpful.

## Transactional Analysis

Like gestalt therapy, transactional analysis is concerned with discovering and fostering self-awareness, genuineness, and responsibility. Both methods are present-oriented. Unlike gestalt therapy, T.A. is interpretive and is generally recognized as being less depth-directed and less emotionally involving.

Transactional analysis provides a frame of reference that most people can understand and put to use in their own lives. Eric Berne has taken key psychoanalytic concepts, such as superego, ego, and id and renamed them "parent," "adult," and "child," respectively. Berne believes that anything that happens between people will involve an interaction between their ego states. T.A. patients are taught to recognize "good" communications, which are complementary, and "bad" ones, which are either "crossed" or "ulterior." For example, if a man comes to group and says, "Boy, I blew my last buck yesterday on the ponies," he is, on an adult-to-adult level, just informing the group of last night's events. However, his general demeanor, his sly smile, indicate that at the ulterior level his "child" is either looking for the "parent" in the others to condone or punish his actions or trying to find another child to play with. Analysis of ego states can become very complicated if pursued to its logical end. Since your "parent" consists of a combination of mother and father, and they in turn had a "parent" which was also made up of two people, and so on, your head is the resting place of an incredibly large number of people.

A person's self-esteem and self-image are conditioned by parental upbringing. If his parents thought well of him, his life script will be positive—like, "You are terrific." If he was handled with animosity and distaste, his life script might be, "You are crazy and disgusting." A person's script is always based on three questions: Who am I? What am I doing here? and What are they doing to me? For example: "I am clever. I am going to go places in the world. Most everyone likes me."

It is the aim of T.A. to make a person aware of his various ego states, transactions, and life scripts so that he can re-program himself and rewrite his drama in accordance with his own wishes. As you can see, most of this is pretty traditional therapy with up-tempo language and emphasis on here-and-now phenomena and interpersonal communications. In order to add a dash of emotionalism, a lot of T.A. practitioners use gestalt methods, such as the two-chair technique.

## Bioenergetic Analysis

According to Alexander Lowen, the originator of this approach to personal growth, each part of the body is the repository of some neurotic problems. By learning to identify specific tensions in parts of the body and by observing a person's posture or gait, the way is opened for a depth exploration of his feelings.

Bioenergetic analysis combines the integration and restructuring of the body with the intellectual understanding of traditional insight-oriented therapy. Lowen has a series of positions and exercises which place a person under ever-increasing physical stress. In one, the patient arches his back over a specially constructed stool—a position that can become excruciatingly painful and lead to involuntary tremor, movements, and vocalizations with recall of early traumatic experiences. Bioenergetic therapists are also fond of having their patients kick or hit pillows and scream as loudly as possible. By letting go in such activities, patients are helped to overcome their fear of the irrational.

Bioenergetics also emphasizes proper breathing. Ideally, the respiratory movements should be neither exaggerated nor shallow; chest, diaphragm, and abdomen should all move harmoniously and rhythmically.

## Primal Therapy

Arthur Janov, in *The Anatomy of Mental Illness,* comments, "What is natural for neurotics is to be defended. Muscles are responding to a stored history of pain. Releasing that history is what cures, not releasing the results of that history." I agree with Janov that attacking muscle bundles in a haphazard fashion is akin to free association: if you stay with it long enough, you may discover something significant. On this basis, many of Lowen's assumptions seem simplistic. Not every person with a hunched-up shoulder is carrying the burdens of the world on his back. In primal therapy, when the patient has relived key primal memories, posture as well as other physical and psychological problems improve or disappear completely.

The core concept of primal therapy is that men and women become neurotic or psychotic because they have been molded, body and mind, into an unnatural state by others. "Primal pain" develops when the child's basic, or primal, needs are not met. The pain increases if he is neither picked up nor allowed to do or say what he wants. Finally, in order to stop hurting, the child must split away or disconnect himself from his needs. This results in his becoming unreal and acquiring a false front designed to please his parents.

The object of primal therapy is to help the individual experience fully those traumatic events and feelings that caused him to become unreal. The technique consists of reawakening early memories in the patient by asking him to go back further and further into his childhood. As he does, the therapist encourages the patient to imagine talking to the significant adults in his past instead of talking about them. In effect this becomes gestalt therapy "then and there" in the "here and now." As the patient regresses, he will experience many bodily tensions, aches, or symptoms; he may develop a pain in his chest or begin to gag. The therapist will reinforce these manifestations by pressing on his chest or helping the patient gag. These physical methods make the experience more vivid and aid in the reliving of the prototypic feelings.

Utilizing these approaches, patients are able to relive events going back to their births and, in some cases, even reexperience what it was like in the womb. Unbelievable as this may sound, it is nonetheless a fact which has been observed, even before Janov, by many reliable investigators.

Primal therapy, in my judgment, is the fastest and most thorough therapeutic tool available for achieving a fundamental personality change. It is a very promising and exciting new approach which may revolutionize therapy in the long run.

## B. INTROSPECTIVE TECHNIQUES

*Fantasy*

When using the technique of fantasy, I ask everyone in the group to imagine finding himself in a certain situation; then I urge them all to see that situation through to its natural end. This is guided fantasy: the leader provides everyone with the same starting point, but each person is allowed to follow his own thoughts. I like fantasies because they offer an easy and rapid access to unconscious material. Also, the contrast between different people's fantasies is ideal material for group interactions.

One of my favorite fantasy exercises is as follows: Lie down and imagine that you're on top of a very tall, tall building. You enter the elevator, and it starts taking you down to the bottom of the building. It is a very safe elevator, and you need not be afraid. It's going down, lower and lower. It passes the main floor, and now it has stopped in the basement. As you get out of the elevator it is very dark, but in the distance you see some light and you move toward it. When you come nearer you notice that this light is above a doorway. You go to the door and open it, and you find yourself in the middle of a huge picture gallery. At the far end of the room there is a sheet draped over a picture. Underneath this

covering is a picture painted by your unconscious. Go over
and take the canvas off and see what your unconscious has
painted. As you look at the picture it might change color or
shape. Keep looking at it until it is completely finished, and
then sit up.

Many patients visualize pictures which are extremely
complicated and revealing of their unconscious. Let me cite
two such examples:

> RALPH: The picture is really a composite of four different
> people, but the face only has two eyes. The two eyes belong
> to all four people, there is one on this side and that's me,
> and there is one on the other side, and that could be any-
> body. And there is a monkey in the back, and all around that
> is a baby. These four parts are all sort of fighting with each
> other.

> THERAPIST: What's the monkey?
> RALPH: It's my anger.

Another person reported the following fantasy:

I see a room with a woman sitting in the middle of it on a
wooden chair. I'll tell you where it comes from. It comes from
the movie *The Snake Pit.* There are snakes crawling back
and forth but the snakes are tied down. Behind her are
people and behind the people there is a door and two
windows. Through the door there is a saloon scene. I can see
a bar and several tables and chairs. On the right side, behind
the window, is a beautiful winter scene, frost and snowy hills,
and on the left-hand side it is mid-summer, green and bright.
The woman in the chair is not old, she's about forty.

Here is another good fantasy exercise. Imagine that
you're home by yourself. Suddenly there is a knock on the

door. You go and open the door. Fantasize as to what will happen from that moment on.

You can make up your own fantasies—about flying carpets or being invisible or being young or very old. By projecting yourself into strange situations, or desired or feared circumstances, you can explore your reactions to fantasies and compare them with reactions of others in the group.

## Visual and Acoustic Exercises

There are a number of exercises which involve exposing the group to music, slides, and other similar stimuli.

Music and poetry can be used for relaxing, setting a mood, triggering off a particular feeling in one person in the group, or as part of a major exercise. I have been collecting records and poems for years now, and I have found them to be extremely helpful in this respect. One of the difficulties with using this medium, however, is that people's tastes differ so enormously. While one person really may be touched by Peggy Lee's "Is That All There Is," someone else may find it and be completely turned off by it.

I think it important to introduce only such literature and music which is free of gimmickry and commercialism. Simon and Garfunkel's "The Sounds of Silence" or "Bridge over Troubled Waters," although they are popular songs, have an honesty about them which makes them almost universally accepted. Rod McKuen's "The Sea" is lovely to listen to when you feel like drifting with your thoughts, but it really turns off people who find the words trite and platitudinous. Classical music such as Vivaldi, Bach, and Beethoven is always helpful as background music to a fantasy or meditation exercise or while the group is painting or sculpting. Spoken records, such as John Donne's "For Whom the Bell Tolls," as read by Orson Welles, may, if played at the right moment, also be very effective.

I have found that T. S. Eliot and James Kavanaugh express the kinds of feelings that group members can empathize with. The latter's "There Are Men Too Gentle to Live Among Wolves" I recommend without reservation. Participants, as a result of listening to poetry or in response to their own emotions, may spontaneously compose their own poems. Here is an example of a poem written in ten minutes during a group session:

> Why are we so alone when we are together?
> What walls separate us?
> I am alone—and that is so real
> My soul seeps out thru my tears.
> But I am still alone
> Not a flower to be looked at—
> to be stepped over or walked around
> or even to be carried
> I do not die when you touch
> But rather come alive
> I am a person to be loved
> To be felt, to be known
> Why am I still alone?

Various slides and pictures can be used similarly to elicit reactions from groups. This technique involves the projection of about ten to fifteen slides that can be expected to have a strong emotional impact—for example, a little boy on a swing, a solitary beach, a coffin, students battling police, or bugs. Each viewer is asked to briefly jot down his immediate response and these are then discussed in the group.

## Art Expression

These techniques include drawing, painting, sculpting, assembling various objects—anything that can be fashioned with your hands into an artistic unit. Participants may be asked to draw themselves or someone else in the group, to fingerpaint their mood, or mold clay into a free form, and then discuss the end product.

One of my favorite art techniques is to place a wide variety of magazines in the center of the room, together with some glue, scissors, pencils, and large sheets of white paper. Then I ask the group members to cut out from the magazines any words, phrases, caricatures, ads, or pictures, which, when assembled and glued to the white sheet, will answer the question, Who Am I? In other words, do a collage.

The wealth of unconscious material that emerges in this process is quite surprising. For some people, their pictures are truly a revelation, and the beauty of the technique is that it requires no interpretation. The person whose collage contains no color at all except one red eye becomes aware of his overpowering feelings of depression and jealousy. Other collages will be so idyllic you can smell phoniness from a mile away; others will have no men or women, or no people at all. This technique is especially well suited for a weekend or time-extended group because, by hanging the collages in the meeting room, the participants are continuously exposed to their unconscious thoughts and feelings.

## Sensory Awareness

Techniques that focus on a person's sense of his own body or that involve the sense of touch, smell, and taste are often referred to as sensory-awareness exercises. They can be done either alone or with one or more persons. Methods such as head tapping, rolling in the grass, running a flower over your partner's face, stretching your partner, and cover-

ing yourself with a sheet and staying there for five minutes
are designed to bring about sensory awakening.

The main thing is to concentrate on what you are doing
and feeling at the time. Most of us either live in the past or
in the future, but rarely do we live in the present. Unless we
learn to live more in the here and now, it is difficult for us to
enjoy life or to relate to others in an authentic way.

*Relaxation and Meditation*

Relaxation exercises are usually used as a prelude to
other techniques, such as fantasy or meditation, though
they can also be used to induce hypnosis or sleep. The
method consists of a series of instructions designed to allow
each part of the body to relax and to empty the mind of its
contents. As one achieves an ever greater state of relaxation,
one gradually begins to float toward slumber.

People often think of meditation as something that is
done in yoga or transcendental meditation, quietly seated
and lost in thought. Actually, there are many forms of meditation; some even involve Japanese martial arts such as
aikido. Most meditation used in growth groups is either
silent and self-directed ("Let's take ten minutes now and
just concentrate on our breathing. Count up to eight to in-
hale and then eight again to exhale. Think of nothing but
the air entering and leaving your body.") or guided. With
some quiet music playing in the background, the leader
might suggest that the group think of what the next five
years have in store for them. Here, relaxation, fantasy, and
meditation all merge, allowing the individual to experience
his feelings. The fact that this is done in a group where people are close to each other increases the impact of these
exercises.

## Self-assessment and Feedback

There are several paper-and-pencil methods for self-assessment, evaluation of the leader and other group members, appraisal of the design of the weekend, and the like. Their most frequent application is in T-groups.

A good example of this technique, and one that is widely used, is the Johari Window. The facilitator draws on a blackboard the following grid:

|  | Known to self | Not known to self |
|---|---|---|
| **Known to others** | I. Area of shared information (Public self) | II. Blind area ("Bad breath" area) |
| **Not known to others** | III. Avoided or hidden area (Private self) | IV. Unknown (Unconscious) |

The leader explains that there are four areas of information about oneself, as represented in the diagram. As a person discloses more of himself to others, his "private self" (area III) decreases in size and area I increases. Under conditions of open feedback his blind area (II) will shrink and area I will expand again. By combining both self-disclosure and feedback, area I can be extended in both directions. Usually area IV remains untouched under these conditions.

The exercise can be made more immediate and gutsy by asking each person to write down on a sheet of paper all the things about himself that he—but no one else in the room—knows (area III). Then these sheets are collected and read out in a random order without disclosing the names of the writers. This can lead to very good and deep interpersonal exchanges.

The following exercise is designed to introduce participants to self-assessment—setting goals, choosing alternatives, selecting resources. They are given paper and pencil and asked to complete the following sentences:

"I am . . . . . . . . . . . . . . . . . . . . . . . . . . . . . . . . . . . . . . . ."

"I need . . . . . . . . . . . . . . . . . . . . . . . . . . . . . . . . . . . . . ."

"I want . . . . . . . . . . . . . . . . . . . . . . . . . . . . . . . . . . . . ."

"I want to become . . . . . . . . . . . . . . . . . . . . . . . . . . . ."

"I need to know . . . . . . . . . . . . . . . . . . . . . . . . . . . . . ."

They are further instructed to write as many completions as possible in about forty-five minutes. Next the participants are encouraged to consider and discuss the various options that are available to them in meeting and pursuing the goals they have listed.

As you may observe, these methods are gentle and allow the group members to move at their own speed. In spite of their lacking "teeth"—or because of it—some people who are very guarded are able to start looking at themselves.

## C. INTERACTIONAL TECHNIQUES

### Confrontation Exercises

These are techniques that are central to encounter groups and other growth groups. They are designed to explore and develop a person's ability to trust, to be intimate, and to take risks.

*The Blind Walk.* Each person is asked to find a partner; then one is blindfolded while the other leads him around the room, through the house, and preferably out of doors. After a half hour they exchange the blindfold and the exercise is repeated. During all this time no one is allowed to talk and all communication must be nonverbal.

Try this exercise. The very fact that you have to select one individual from among ten others is anxiety-producing. Many encounter techniques involve this type of choice because it affords you an opportunity to act in your characteristic way. We usually do not do what we would really like to do. During the exercise you will find that some people are very gentle and creative while others show little regard for the safety of the person they are leading. Some partners pull and shove when their "charge" is not yet ready to move. The person who is blindfolded becomes acutely aware of his other senses and is often struck by the extent of his dependency on his seeing partner. Once everyone has finished the exercise, the group members dwell at length on their thoughts and feelings. Sometimes this exercise alone can provide enough material for hours of meaningful interaction. It is especially well suited for a Friday or Saturday night of a weekend marathon in the country.

*Mirroring.* This exercise often brings two people very close to each other. Hold up your palms against the palms of your partner, who is sitting across from you and, without actually touching, move in unison. First, one of you plays the leader and does motions with his hands while the other follows and then you reverse roles. You very soon begin to feel all sorts of emotions, such as embarrassment, joy, and attraction for your partner. Once the exercise is over, discuss your feelings with each other, and, if you desire, with the group.

*Risk Taking.* After the group members have developed a good deal of trust in each other, the leader may suggest that during the next few hours everyone in the group should do or say something he considers risky. The exercise will get off the ground faster if the leader initiates it. People have many actions or thoughts they are afraid to express because they expect rejection or ridicule from the group. This exercise usually elicits revelations about a person's sexual practices or fantasies that he has been unable to confide to the group. It may also involve asking for some "stroking" from a member of the opposite sex: "May I go for a walk with you? May I hold you in my arms?" Often, just being able to talk about one's deep, dark secrets or being able to ask for something is, in itself, extremely helpful to the person. The next thing he learns is that his catastrophic expectations do not come true. The group does not laugh at him or ostracize him because he screwed a sheep at the age of twelve, nor does the girl he wants to kiss slap him or tell him what a dirty old man he is.

All these techniques involve close contact with another person and encourage the patient to reach out to others. There are a lot of people who have experienced the breakup of a very precious and loving relationship in the past and have not reached out since. Rather than risk being hurt again, they have permanently shut themselves off from all relationships which could conceivably lead to another close bond and another rejection. Their reaction, although easily understandable, sentences them to a life of loneliness and isolation. It is the belief of the encounter group movement that it is better to reach out and be rejected, even repeatedly, than never to reach out and thus forfeit the opportunity to experience acceptance and fulfillment.

## Role Playing

This technique differs from psychodrama in that it is not elaborately staged. Great use is made of fantasied situations in which the various group members interact.

*Hidden Agendas.* Half of the group volunteers to play predetermined roles; the other half acts as observers. Each role player receives individual instruction from the trainer as to his position on a certain issue—for example, campus unrest over the firing of a certain instructor. One person plays the instructor, another the dean of the college, another a representative of the student council, and so on. Each comes to a meeting called by the dean with specific objectives known only to him. Each only introduces himself, and the dean starts the meeting. After a predetermined time, the members reveal their true goals and commence to discuss how hidden agendas affected their interactions and the feelings that surfaced during the discussion.

*Robinson Crusoe.* Each person pairs off with someone in the group. One person is designated as A, the other as B. A has been washed up on a large, barren island. He has a loaded gun and sufficient food to last him ten days. The next day person B is washed up on the beach. B approaches A and asks for food. Take it from there.

After about ten minutes, when A and B have resolved the conflict—A shares his food, or refuses, or B attacks him and gets shot in the process—we provide an additional piece of information. The day after B arrives on the island he finds a cave with a huge supply of canned food, tents, and other military hardware. What does he do?

*Odd Man Out.* I recommend this one only for seasoned veterans of encounter groups. Select, nonverbally, two people in the group whom you feel are most unlike you. In response to such questions as "What do you mean?" the instructions are repeated and the group is told to interpret them any way it wishes. If more than two people want the same person, a physical struggle may develop, or one of the three may give in and move over, or someone else may help to tear a person away. Sooner or later the group divides into triads. If the number of people is not divisible by three, you form three groups of three and one of four, and so on. The members of the small groups are invited to discuss among themselves why each chose the other two and how they feel about their choices. This may take about twenty minutes.

During the next twenty minutes each triad is asked to define a meaningful criterion which, if applied to their group, would make one person stand out as different from the other two. By "meaningful" we do not mean a physical quality, such as color of hair or height, but a personality characteristic, such as sense of humor, hostility, or warmth. The person who proves to be different (the other two are more alike than he according to the criterion selected) will be ejected from the group and required to sit in the center of the room together with the other "odd men out."

The last part of the formal exercise consists of giving the ejectees a number of choices. They can form their own group, return to their own group, switch to another group, or do anything else that they would like to do except leave the room. Once they have exercised their options (most of them return to their original groups) a brief discussion follows in the small groups exploring the participants' feelings. After sufficient time has elapsed the group members reassemble and share their experiences.

If the instructions are given in stages and are clearly explained, this is not as complicated an exercise as it might appear on first reading. It is, however, anxiety-provoking, so if you want to get a little excitement going, this technique will do nicely! The ejection part, especially, produces feelings of rejection in many participants. Some people will volunteer to leave the group right away rather than wait to be kicked out. You may even have two individuals vying for the privilege of leaving the group, which, almost by definition, makes the third person different from them and naturally forces him to leave. Because this exercise puts considerable strain on one's relationship with some members of the group, it must be done when there is a lot of time still available to heal the wounds.

These exercises are valuable because the participants become so engrossed in playing out their roles or fantasies that their normal watchful stance is weakened and some of their true characteristics brake through their defensive masks. Besides, they provide some change from the sitting-around-the-circle-and-discussing-our-problems routine.

*Physical-Contact "Games"*

These "games" are often intended to serve as icebreakers or as an outlet for pent-up physical energy after a long session. No matter how much laughter they elicit, they all have serious undertones, and some of them are quite forceful in making people aware of their bodies and their reactions to other bodies.

*The People Machine.* A person from the group starts moving about the room and makes a sound. Another person may place one arm on the first individual's shoulder and begin to bob his head while emitting a hissing sound. The next person attaches himself to the second and makes a distinct motion and sound, and then the next, until everyone forms one large, moving, shouting heap of people.

*The Steam Roller.* This is a similar exercise, but with a great deal of subtle meaning. It involves asking all members of the group to lie down beside each other on their stomachs, head to toe. The first one is instructed to crawl over the bodies of his buddies and then lie down next to the last person in the line. The exercise is repeated until everyone has had a turn. Following that, the participants are requested to turn on their backs and the activity is repeated as before. Because the group members are lying head to toe, each person is pretty well forced to crawl over chests and stomachs. Naturally, this produces some sexual feelings or thoughts of sex, which are then aired in the group.

*Body Lift.* I usually do this beautiful exercise in two phases. In phase one, one person lies, face down, in the middle of the room. Half of the group kneels down at his right side and the other at his left. They gently begin to slap his body, increasing and decreasing the rhythm. Then they turn the person over and slowly pick him up as if they were cradling a child. They may lift him high above their heads and then let him sink to their waists and repeat that several times, or just rock him back and forth for a few minutes and then put him down. I know of no one who has tried this exercise and did not like it.

Techniques such as these help people relax and trust each other. Physical contact is so taboo in our society that once that barrier is removed all other obstacles to open communication appear to be less formidable. The group leader's participation in these activities will put the seal of approval on them and sanctify them. So it is important that he show no reluctance in taking part, otherwise the group will also hesitate and the whole exercise may flop.

## Massage

Most North Americans are painfully afraid of touching each other. They have to walk a tightrope between four hundred years of Puritan repression and the blatant exploitation of sex. They are usually afraid that the world will misinterpret their most innocent gesture as a sexual advance. Some of this anxiety is of course due to projection: the drive to sexualize the relationship conflicts with the injunction of the superego, which says, "You dirty little boy, you ought to be ashamed of yourself."

Little boys and girls engage in exploratory sexual activities by playing doctor and nurse. Doctors, nurses, hairdressers, and tailors are licensed by society to physically touch their clients. However, they must do so on a cold, impersonal level, which is equated with professionalism.

There is a wide spectrum of human feelings—pleasurable, sensual feelings—between physical therapy (massage) and intercourse. Massage will make you tingle more than a haircut and less than an embrace. It is a beautiful sensual experience that is easily learned.

I ask the group members to get into their bathing suits and select a partner they would like to work with. One of the partners lies down on a large towel. The other warms some massage oil in his hands and spreads it over those areas of his partner's body to be massaged. Any vegetable oil, with the exception of corn oil or peanut oil, makes a fine base. Coconut oil and safflower oil are highly recommended; you can get your druggist to scent them with an essence extract like roses or cinnamon or a perfume. Scent, music, lighting, and cleanliness are determinant factors in making this a memorable experience. Any laughter or loud chatter spoils the mood. If someone is present who does not wish to participate, make sure that he does not disturb the rest.

I usually demonstrate and explain each stroke in turn, first for one group of masseurs and then for the next. I concentrate on the face, neck, shoulders, and head. If some of the group members at the end of the session wish to proceed and massage each other's backs or legs, they are free to do so. (There is a thorough exposition of the various strokes in *The Art of Sensual Massage* by Gordon Inkeles and Murray Todris.)

Those who have never received a massage respond to it with pleasurable amazement. They feel relaxed and have warm feelings for the person who massaged them. They enjoy both the giving and receiving of pleasure—which they are surprised to experience apart from sexual feelings. It is as if the realization that they can touch another person without becoming sexually intimate relieved them of a huge burden.

What is the rationale for using massage in a group setting? Because being touched by another person mobilizes memories from early childhood days and because of its sexual connotations, massaging often triggers some pretty strong feelings in people. I often introduce this technique on a Saturday night of a weekend marathon and then reserve Sunday morning for a discussion of the participants' different reactions. Those group members who so desire may obtain mimeographed copies of the massage instructions. This will enable them to continue to practice the art of massage on their friends and spouses.

## Summing Up

Techniques borrowed from the theater, the arts, meditation, and physical training, have been adapted for the purpose of aiding people to become more aware of their emotions and bodies. We have reviewed and classified some of the best-known exercises used in growth groups.

# VIII

# The Group Marathon

Marathon sessions are used extensively by growth groups. Although each group leader has his own definition of a marathon, generally it is a continuous group meeting of at least six hours and no more than forty-eight hours. In some marathons there is no provision for sleep or rest; all meals are taken within the group; and you are allowed to leave the meeting room only to use the washroom. Other marathons have time allotted for rest and recreation—of these the most popular form is the weekend group. I shall use the latter as the prototype for this discussion.

The weekend marathon usually starts on a Friday night and ends on Sunday afternoon. The reasons for holding a group session on a weekend are self-evident: both the group leader and the members are free of occupational obligations, and participants who have children can have them looked after by their spouses. The ideal location is outside the city but preferably no more than two hours driving distance from it. Religious retreats, resort lodges, farms, or a member's cottage may serve the purpose very well. The accommodation will vary from the extremely luxurious (NTL executives lab) to the most rustic, where group members are expected to bring sleeping bags and cook their own meals.

Marathon encounter participants are usually strangers to each other. Many psychiatrists and psychologists conduct marathons for their individual or group patients. Naturally, these people have known each other, and they will have access to continued help (if they so desire), which the "one-shot" encounter groups lack as a rule.

What are the advantages to the marathon approach as opposed to weekly or biweekly two-and-a-half hour group meetings? Perhaps the best way to answer the question is to examine four important parameters of time-extended groups. These are:

1. The setting
2. The time element
3. Informal activities
4. Role of the group leader

## The Setting

By removing themselves from their work and family ties, participants temporarily submerge their reality concerns, and their intrapersonal and interpersonal problems come to the fore. Participants are forced by circumstances literally to live with each other for two days and two nights. While many people have no difficulty keeping their defenses intact for an hour or two, after ten hours on a weekend their true selves begin to show through. When this happens, they often become very anxious and wish to leave. But the fact that they have driven, let us say, an hour to attend the marathon, that they have paid a fee, and that they would have to drive back on their own or take a bus or train, all militate against their leaving. In the city, if they wished to leave, they would simply take a cab and forget about the group. More than once I have seen people stay in a group simply because it was too much trouble to leave.

The rural setting is also helpful because it represents neutral territory; unlike his office, the site is not linked in the participants' minds with the leader. Here, all are outsiders and in that sense equal. This helps the group leader shed his authoritarian role and become more a part of the group. The great distance between leader and members is decreased, and a feeling of warmth and cohesiveness within the group is created.

The combination of intensive group sessions followed by periods of quiet solitude, rest, or informal camaraderie makes the weekend marathon, in my opinion, a much more complete and emotionally satisfying experience than the continuous eighteen to twenty-four hour marathon.

## The Time Element

Most group leaders who conduct weekend marathons adopt something like the following routine for group sessions. About eighteen to twenty-four hours of formal group work are divided as follows:

Friday—8 PM to 11 PM
Saturday—9 AM to 12 noon
Saturday—2 PM to 6 PM

Saturday—8 PM to 12 PM
Sunday—9 AM to 12 noon
Sunday—2 PM to 4 PM

Because the guillotine of the advancing clock, ever present in the office, is virtually absent at the marathon, participants feel less inhibited to deal with material they would consider too time-consuming for office meetings.

Often, interpersonal conflicts which have been smoldering in an ongoing group for a long time are suddenly unearthed. Patients who have been harboring resentments or have some serious doubts as to the therapist's competence or integrity begin to talk about them. Consequently, many hostile feelings are resolved at an early stage in the weekend and do not interfere later with efforts at reaching deeper levels of understanding.

The open-endedness of these sessions allows those members of the group who are neither the most articulate nor saddled with the most pressing external problems to talk about their concerns. In regular weekly sessions such individuals hardly ever get any air time. Furthermore, situations arise where a person needs two or three hours of continuous help from the group before he can achieve an emotional breakthrough. It is virtually impossible to give one member of a group of eight or ten people this sort of attention except on a marathon.

As the group approaches the designated end of the weekend, pressure to become involved and to achieve their goals begins to build up in participants who have not yet been "on." The realization that they had almost unlimited time at their disposal and yet "blew it" acts as a powerful motivating force for self-exploration, either during the time that's still left or at least in the near future.

Because of the amount of time and indoor and outdoor

space that is available, the therapist is free to introduce a wide variety of techniques that in his judgment are beneficial to the group. Some of these techniques, either because they evoke deep and protracted feeling responses or because they require a lot of time to execute, cannot be utilized in weekly sessions. Their use on the weekend acts as a strong catalyst to the development and identification of significant emotional material.

# Informal Activities

As you have observed from the timetable at the start of this chapter, the participants have a fair amount of free time to spend as they like. Some will go to sleep; others listen to records, take walks, or play chess. Much of what happens during these informal activities filters back to the group later with astonishing results.

I recall recently joining two men and a woman from our group for a stroll through the woods. It was, for me, a very uneventful walk and after about twenty minutes we returned to the lodge. During the session, I learned that one of the men was, during the whole walk, terribly afraid he would touch me. The other felt he was babbling like an idiot. The female member of the trio said she would have liked to talk with me alone and was afraid I would laugh at her feelings. And that was only the surface of the iceberg!

We all know that mealtime plays an important role in the development of children, and yet this aspect of a person's life is hardly ever explored in the more traditional forms of group work. The way people help to serve meals and eat provides a wealth of information. How they sit and talk, how they walk—whether they lag behind or rush ahead—

their toilet habits, and their sleepwear all tell volumes. During weekly office visits we have no access to these observations.

## The Role of the Leader

A few years ago Jay Haley wrote a paper, entitled "The Art of Being a Failure as a Therapist." He concluded his article by listing the five Bs of Dynamic Failure:

1. Be passive
2. Be inactive
3. Be reflective
4. Be silent
5. Beware

It is difficult to conduct groups and abide by these five Bs. To remain passive, inactive, and silent on a marathon is just about impossible for a leader. Furthermore, the surprising discovery that I and many of my colleagues have made is that the less we play at being "the therapist," the more we are ourselves, the more real we are, the more truly therapeutic we become.

I am convinced that role playing by the therapist only encourages role playing by the patient. On the other hand, the leader's willingness to risk himself and thus become vulnerable enables the group to do likewise. I find the practice of many therapists who expect total self-disclosure from their patients without ever saying anything about themselves completely indefensible, both on theoretical and ethical grounds.

One of the difficulties for the therapist under these conditions is that, as the group sees so much of him, they may learn to know him too well. He may reveal to them facts about his life or aspects of his character which are not to their total liking. He may occasionally be insensitive, commit faux pas, or make an outright therapeutic blunder. Such occurrences are for anyone hard to take, and no leader will particularly enjoy looking silly. Nonetheless, group members are able to see their leader now as a human being instead of as some ephemeral creature way above "the rest of us common peasants." Thus, instead of constantly trying to topple him from his pedestal or taking pot shots at him to see if he will bleed when cut, they can join him in a cooperative venture toward mutual growth.

# The Marathon as Drama in Three Acts

The marathon experience, like good drama, consists of a beginning, a middle, and an end. These three acts are distinct and separate; they are characterized by different themes, moods, and behavior. By studying each phase in turn, I hope to give the uninitiated a better understanding of what happens at a typical marathon and to give the expert some new ideas—both practical and theoretical—about conducting marathons.

## PHASE I

This phase is characterized by a high level of anxiety. All participants are either afraid that something terrible is going to happen to them or that the good things they are hoping to gain from the weekend will not materialize.

Let us listen in on one such group:

THERAPIST: Let's talk about all the fears and expectations that people usually bring with them to a weekend of this sort.

WALTER: Well, two things, one is that I decided not to smoke during the sessions and I'm not going to. The other thing was that several times I caught myself programming ahead; I want to do this or I'm going to try that—and I've stopped myself doing that—and there is only one thing that I really want to do and that is to be as open as I possibly can be about what's going on here [pointing to his gut].

KENT: When you said to bring bathing suits along I thought, Oh God—you see I'm not too proud of my figure —I was a bit uptight about that. It also brought to mind my sort of sexual inferiority feelings. That's about it, I was excited to come.

THERAPIST: Elsa, you looked dubious when he said he was excited about coming here.

ELSA: Well, I think Kent would be excited about coming here. He seems to have thrown himself into the group as much as I've ever seen anybody do that. I wasn't excited, I thought to myself, 'Well we are all set for the Alfred Hitchcock movie.' I don't feel very comfortable at the thought of a weekend with strange people. I realize how important the thing could be, but I don't know whether I can live up to it— be as open as I should be.

KENT [to Barb]: How do you feel? Because you were terrified.

BARB: I can't stand going away on weekends. If I have to see people for an extended period of time, they get awfully fed up with me.

EMILY: I feel bloody uptight too. Like I said to myself too, I would like to know what my real problem is and I'm going to find out this weekend. Right now I can't even think clearly. What I'm doing at school, I find is not effective, so I'll either have to find out what it is about my work that is not good or I'll have to stop doing it.

WALTER: Is your work ineffective in your terms or in somebody else's terms?

EMILY: Well in my terms.

FRANK: Well, I feel that all the things that you do . . .

THERAPIST: That you do?

FRANK: That I do, are to improve myself without pills. Something that I do to improve myself, O.K.? I felt about this weekend that I will go up, but I'm pretty sure that nothing is going to happen. The more I think about it that's the way I feel. On one hand I would like a lot to happen and on the other hand there's something in me that's saying no, nothing is going to happen.

THERAPIST: In other words, let's not look forward to it because if something happens I'll be disappointed.

FRANK: Maybe. I'm not sure.

AGNES: Or I might not let anything happen?

FRANK: Oh, I never considered that. I've considered that I will try. One expectation I have is that it will give me enough strength and confidence to go through an interview that I have coming up on Monday.

THERAPIST: And you all know that Edith is not going to be here, because on Wednesday she was in a minor car accident, and suffered a bruised elbow. On Thursday she gave me a call saying that she had a slight headache and she was not going to be able to come to the weekend. When I insisted that this really was no reason for not coming to the weekend she said she'll see what she can do. And then on Thursday night she called me and she said that she told her mother that she is going to spend the weekend with some friends in the country, and her mother insisted that she should come home and spend the weekend with her, and not with her friends, especially now that she had this injury. And when I told Edith to tell her mother that she wouldn't do that, Edith said that she was sorry but she just could not hurt her mother by not following her advice. I pointed out to Edith that one of her major problems was her relationship with her mother, that she was a thirty-year-old professional girl who was still being told by her mother who she should go out with and how she should spend her weekends, and that this would be a good first attempt at getting away from mother. And Edith said that she knew all that but she just could not hurt her mother's feelings, and that she was not coming to the weekend.

AGNES: Well, I know that she was very scared to come to the weekend, and I guess this is her way out, isn't it?

EARL [taking out a piece of paper]: My wife packed my suitcase for me and this was at the bottom of it. It says, 'Thoughts on the departure of a loved one on a weekend with a suspect shrink and nine psychos. If you find the weekend taxing,/that you call relaxing,/and other peoples' freak-outs get you down,/If they say we are not happy,/our marriage is sure crappy/and we should split before our egos drown,/Take heart my adult lover,/there is hope, I'm not your mother,/or even the father who you half forgot./In spite of how they psych you,/you will find that I still like you./Love, Ann.'

WALTER: She sounds kind of apprehensive, doesn't she?

EARL: Yeah, yeah. Well she knows that the group has quite an effect on me on Tuesday nights and I guess a weekend will be that much worse.

WALTER: Do you both look upon your involvement here as a threat to your marriage?

EARL: No, not really. She just doesn't want the group to come between us. My wife is really all I've got.

EMILY: Is there some doubt in your mind that your marriage is good or that it will last.

WALTER: No, none whatsoever.

In another group one lady brought two books along. When she was questioned about why she always had at least one book with her during the sessions, she said that she felt guilty enough about coming to the weekend instead of spending it with her family, and that the least she could do during the weekend was to read two books. The group members pointed out to her that she was doing something—she was coming for therapy, she was trying to straighten herself out, and that in itself should be sufficient. When the subject was pursued further by the group she said, "Well really I would prefer if I were knitting some socks instead of reading, that really would be more useful." She completely avoided coming to terms with the problem of her guilt. She did not explain why she felt she did not deserve to go away for the weekend without having something concrete to show for it— like a pair of knitted socks or at least two books read. When asked why she went around feeling guilty, she replied, "Because that's a trait of mind." Which of course is no answer at all.

People like Elsa and Edith in the first group or the lady with the books do not tend to benefit much from a marathon. Trying to communicate with them about feelings is futile. They are too busy shoring up their defenses to participate in the group process. To a lesser degree, the same applies to people who say they are attending because they heard that marathons are interesting experiences. When questioned as to the specifics of their expectations they usually reply in the negative, "I have none. I am just here to see what will happen." In point of fact they want to prove that they are O.K., that they have no problems. And they will make sure that no one shatters this self-image, even if it should prove to be an illusion.

Most leaders will start the group off by asking each member what he or she hopes to gain from the weekend. This little exercise serves to unfreeze people. The first words are always the hardest to say; by answering the question the ice is broken. Moreover, the answers provide important material for further discussion—for example, when Kent mentions his sexual inferiority feelings or when Barb says that people "get awfully fed up" with her, etc.

If, after everyone has had his turn, a freewheeling interchange occurs, the group is off to a good start. Should the group come to a halt after a few minutes, another exercise using smaller groups may be introduced; most people, after all, feel more comfortable with one or two strangers than with ten. These triads may be given pencils and paper and asked to write down all the names they have ever been called. This includes first names, last names, diminutives, nicknames, titles, swear words—anything at all that has stuck in their minds. When all three have completed their lists, each person in turn reads out what he has written and answers questions about it. If a person gets to sit with two sensitive people, this technique can quickly help him recall memories charged with strong feelings. After about half an hour, the large group is reconvened and members are asked for their reactions. Since, by then, everyone has had a good chance to talk and has befriended at least two other people in the group, the discussion becomes more lively and less dependent on the leader.

## PHASE II

This phase begins on Saturday morning and lasts to about Sunday morning or Sunday noon. The group knows that this is it. The previous night the preliminary skirmishes took place, but on Saturday the real battle is fought.

A typical day may proceed as follows. The morning ma

start off with the leader asking for any thoughts or feelings from last evening or anything of significance that may have occurred during the night. This usually does not take too long because the first night the group does not stay up late. Also, participants are still wary of each other. The therapist may then choose to allow the group to develop at its own rate, or he may wish to quicken the pace by using a technique that will encourage interaction.

I have described one such technique, "Odd Man Out," in the chapter on techniques. Here is another you may wish to know about: Imagine you are on board a ship. Suddenly, in the middle of the night, there is a storm; you are awakened and told to get into a lifeboat. You have no idea where you are. You are told that there is an island a few miles ahead and that you may choose two people from this group to go with you in the boat. Select, nonverbally, the two members of this group who, in your opinion, will help you survive best, both physically and emotionally, on this unknown island. Do not worry about the other participants; they will be picked up and rescued. The persons you choose must, of course, in turn see you as helpful to them; otherwise they can go with someone else. In other words, each member of the triad agrees to be with the other two. Once you arrive on the island, discuss why you have chosen the individuals you are with, what you would do on the island in the short and the long run, and what sort of personality problems, if any, you foresee developing among yourselves.

Many people become extremely engrossed in this exercise. They find that the island community they have created is really much better than their present life arrangements. They enjoy each other's company, share the labor, the sex— everything—and live an idyllic existence. Others are not able to get very far into the fantasy and soon begin to talk of trivialities.

Some group members just sit and wait to be chosen, while others move actively to do the choosing at the start. Some voice strong opinions on the island; others remain passive. A few individuals surprise everyone with their resourcefulness and inventiveness. They know how to make a fire, build a raft, and plant wheat. Others feel completely lost without a supermarket. The variations of reactions are infinite and give rise to a lot of animated discussion when everyone gets back into the total group.

Saturday afternoon, especially if the weather is favorable, is a good time to get outside and engage in physical activities. Such techniques as the Blind Walk, Mirroring, the People Machine, the Steam Roller, Trust Exercises, and the like, lend themselves well to nonanxiety-producing body contact and sensory-awareness purposes. It seems essential for purposes of establishing a climate of total trust that participants experience their own bodies and those of others. People, otherwise, are too reticent to really let loose with their feelings as the marathon progresses. Indeed, the sooner one can get the group to interact on a physical, nonsexual, level the better.

In my experience the warmth of the group is largely influenced by its female members. Since women are allowed by society to be more emotional and to do more touching than men, they will generally precede the men in breaking down—crying, dancing for sheer joy, touching people as they pass them. This emotionality and warmth then becomes contagious, and soon almost everyone is affected by it. If the women in the group are withdrawn and emotionally aloof and the men are that way too, it becomes much more difficult to unite these separate individuals into a cohesive, cooperative unit. The techniques described above are aimed at decreasing inhibitions and overcoming defensiveness.

Saturday night is "The Really Big Show." I spoke previously of orchestrating the group weekend. I see to the thorough planning and selection of the setting: the techniques, the music, the poetry, even the clothes that we all should wear (old and informal, such as jeans, turtle-necks, etc.). All are necessary ingredients to a successful marathon.

I can hear you asking: But what is a successful marathon? A successful marathon is one which provides all its members with growth-inducing experiences. It does not need to be highly charged—we can do without thunder and lightning—but it does require the deepest involvement of as many members of the group as possible. Once they participate and begin to care about each other, the rest will follow naturally.

The evening, or part of the evening, may be devoted to a series of exercises done in dyads. The group leader asks each person to find a partner, preferably of the opposite sex, with whom he or she will work for most of the evening. They are advised to choose a person they feel quite comfortable with. Then they are instructed to kneel behind their partner, hold his hands and conduct to music. After a few minutes the partners change position.

In the next exercise partner A lies on his back while B sits behind his head, picks up A's head in both hands and gently rotates it from left to right and back three times.

Both of these exercises are deceptive. They appear simple, yet they tell a lot about a person, particularly in terms of control, dependence, and independence. There are some people who constantly anticipate the move of their partner or who cannot allow themselves to be handled by another. Also, holding a person's head in one's hands is for some people a very strange experience. They are afraid of dropping it or crushing it. Many are surprised at how light it is.

If we wish to encourage a more intimate encounter, we can use the following series of exercises:

Listen to your partner's stomach.

Now listen to his heart.

Look into your partner's eyes and think of the following:

How would you feel looking after this person in sickness?

How would you feel working with him?

Tell your partner what part of your body you like the least.

How does sex embarrass you?

If you had twenty-four hours with this person, how would you spend it?

These interchanges are always very open and sincere and help people to talk about the kinds of things they really wanted to talk about all along. When this exercise is going well, I find it best not to interrupt the flow by going back into the large group but rather to move into massaging or guided meditation right away.

At the conclusion of the evening we play records, have some wine and cheese, and just bask in our mutual good feelings. People gradually drift off to their bedrooms, although a few hardy types often stay up talking all night.

Sunday morning I ask the participants whether they have any feelings about Saturday night that they would like to share with the other members. Sometimes the question, "What would you do if you had another evening to spend here?" elicits provocative answers. By now the group has gained momentum; it not only does not require "priming the pump" but would likely resent the use of techniques. So unless specifically called for, I find it advisable not to interfere with the group process in any major way at this point.

Before breaking up at noon, I will suggest to the group members (if this seems appropriate) that after lunch they take a silent walk with someone from the group. On their walk they are to look for a present—a flower, a stone, a branch—that they would like to give to one or more people in the group.

At two o'clock, when we reconvene, we talk about the walk and exchange presents. I have performed this exercise many times, and it never ceases to amaze me how truly beautiful, warm, and creative people can be. For example, a woman gave a burr to a man in the group because he "put a burr in my saddle and made me run faster." Occasionally a caterpillar in a cocoon or an acorn is presented; both symbolize the donor's belief that the person receiving the gift is capable of considerable growth. One girl on a recent weekend gave me a robin's egg dedicated "to the only person who did not lay an egg this weekend."

This final exercise stimulates everyone to reflect on what has happened to him during the marathon. Objectives are formulated for the future and plans are made for reunions. The group members often express the feeling that they have never before experienced this warmth and closeness toward anyone—let alone a group—in their whole life.

My present to the group usually consists of a poem, read aloud, that I have found particularly meaningful to me. The one below is from a greeting card I recently received:

> What is real
> asked the Rabbit one day
> When they were lying
> side by side
> Does it mean having things buzz inside you
> and a stick out handle
> Real isn't how you're made
> said the Skin Horse
> It's a thing that happens to you
> When a child loves you for a long long time
> not just to play with, but Really loves you
> then you become real
> Does it hurt? asked the Rabbit.
> Sometimes, said the Skin Horse for he was always
>     truthful
> When you are Real you don't mind being hurt.

> Does it happen all at once, like being wound up
>     or bit by bit.
> It doesn't happen all at once. You become. It
>     takes
> a long time. That's why it doesn't often happen
> to people who break easily, or who have sharp
>     edges,
> or have to be carefully kept. Generally, by the
>     time
> you are Real, most of your hair has been loved off
> and your eyes drop out and you get loose at the
>     joints
> and very shabby.
> But these things don't matter at all once you
>     are Real
> You can't be ugly, except to people
> Who don't understand.[1]

M. Williams

Then I ask the group members to lie down in the middle
of the room with their heads toward the center and tell them
an allegory called "The Transfer."

> Eric was sitting in the middle of the streetcar, and oppo-
> site him there was an elegant, elderly gentleman. At the
> first stop several people got on and hurried to the center in
> order to get a seat. But none was vacant. The first person
> who came from one side was a well-dressed, elderly lady;
> the first person from the other side was a little old woman
> who was carrying a bundle of kindling wood on her shoul-
> der. The elegant gentleman sitting opposite Eric jumped
> up in order to make room for the well-dressed lady. But
> at the last moment he noticed that the old lady with the
> sticks was about to slip into the vacant seat behind his

---

[1] Margery Williams, *The Velveteen Rabbit*, Doubleday & Company, Inc., Garden City, New York, 1958.

back, and he blocked her path. The well-dressed lady, who had reached the seat, gave him a smile, whereupon he tipped his hat and she sat down.

After a few seconds, during which the three people concerned began to settle down in their new positions— the old woman put her bundle on the floor, the gentleman put on his gloves and reached for one of the straps, the well-dressed lady pulled her coat down over her knees— after a few seconds, then, Eric got up and offered his seat to the old lady with the wood.

She was a bit surprised, but sat down immediately, and after she had put her bundle to her knees, she moved her hard hand up to Eric's face and stroked his cheek.

Eric blushed and looked to the left and to the right to see if anyone had noticed it, for he had not wanted the caress. Now the well-dressed lady stood up and offered her seat to the old woman. But since this would only have meant a change of seat for the old woman, she stayed put, but also stroked the well-dressed lady's cheek. Dazed, the elegant lady offered her seat to the elegant gentleman who had given it up for her, but he refused to sit down again. She offered her seat to Eric, and perhaps because he also declined her offer, she stroked his cheek. She also stroked the cheek of the elegant gentleman and then Eric's again. Thereupon a plain gentleman who had the window seat next to the well-dressed lady jumped up and offered his seat to her. Then the young lady who was sitting next to the woman with the bundle offered her window seat to her, and Eric could not resist the temptation to stroke this young lady's cheek. Smiling the young lady stroked the cheek of the old woman who had refused her offer, and then turning, she bent far over the back of her seat toward the people on the back seats and stroked the cheeks of two of them.

Suddenly it was impossible to keep the activity confined to the center group of seats, and people on the entire streetcar began to stroke one another and offer one another their seats. Nobody wanted to sit down anymore; but still, some people kept getting pushed down into seats. They arose again the moment they thought themselves unobserved, and mingled with the tender jostling of the standees. All had their cheeks stroked, everybody stroked somebody else's cheek, and finally all were standing and all the seats were unoccupied. Even the old woman with the wood had stood up held her bundle in one arm, and used her other hand to participate in the caresses which everybody was bestowing with great feeling. She joined gladly, for after all, she had started it.

At length someone had the idea of letting the ticket conductor sit down; he had already been stroked several times, albeit with some reserve, because he was an official. No sooner had this idea been expressed than combined forces pushed him down into a seat, and he was stroked with such rapidity that he threatened the many people crowding him if they did not at least let him pull the signal cord for the streetcar to proceed.

They reached the next stop, which was the busiest transfer point in town, and this was where everybody got off. They assembled together outside and waved to the conductor; the elegant gentleman even tossed him a rather large bill. They exchanged addresses, so that finally everybody had everybody else's address.

During all this they continued to stroke one another undisturbed, and the first people who had to leave stroked the strangers they met in the street. But these people did not understand, get angry, said something about liquor and lunatics, and the next passersby who were stroked by the ex-passengers even blazed into fight with them. This so intimidated the ex-streetcar group that they no longer dared to stroke one another's faces, but only stroked hands, and when Eric did stroke the cheek of the young lady who had sat first next to him and then next to the woman with the bundle, she even slapped his face.

That ended it all. The only things left were a few slips

with addresses which people had dropped, as well as a few visiting cards, and even these scattered when a light breeze blew over them.

I then remind the group members that those they have left behind in the city were not part of this experience and will not be able to fully appreciate it. Do not get upset when you arrive home and your wife asks you, "Did you have fun?" As a matter of fact, on returning to your family you would be well advised not to discuss the weekend. Ask your wife, rather, what she and the children did, whether it was difficult for them to manage without you. Nothing tends to destroy the marathon faster than a huge argument as soon as you enter the house. So be prepared for this eventuality and avoid it. The weekend need not end like the streetcar passengers' short journey.

I conclude the session by playing a song or two— Melanie's "The Saddest Thing" and "Beautiful People," or The Moody Blues "Burn Slowly the Candle of Life"—while the group remains closely huddled and holding hands.

# The Afterglow

If the participants are carefully prepared for "re-entry," then the chances for a hard landing are considerably lessened. Many people in the past have come to regard the whole marathon experience as divorced from reality, because a few hours or days following it they become enmeshed in bitter disputes with their friends or colleagues. As a result, all the good feelings and resolutions they made during the weekend evaporated, and they felt as if the marathon had never really happened. Indeed, they felt worse than if it had never happened because they felt betrayed, conned.

Keep in mind that it is not possible to correct in twenty hours what it took a lifetime to put out of alignment. The most that the marathon can hope to accomplish is to begin for the participant a process of self-reevaluation and self-renewal. It may help the individual to get some feedback as to how he is perceived by others and how he compares with others.

Here is a very brief transcript of a follow-up session:

DANNY: I have never in my entire life felt so high as I have for the past week following the weekend. In looking back on it, I'm forced to the conclusion that the reason I felt so good was that here are eight or ten people who I can care about and who can care about me, and we'll band together in this life and we'll go hand in hand through the trials and tribulations of life. When my feelings simmered down, I realized that that's not quite so. You can't live for me, you can't support me, you can't make my decisions. I'm ultimately still alone. I think realizing that has to be part of coming down from a weekend. I've realized during the last few days that my depressions were an expression of my need for wanting to be loved and cared for. To be cherished, to be protected, to not have to face it all. . .

THERAPIST: By yourself.

DANNY: That's right, by myself.

JAN: Which was the elation that you were talking about a minute ago. That for a brief time you felt that there were some people who would help you face the loneliness.

I would like to conclude my discussion of the positive aspects of the marathon with two letters from members of a T-group I conducted for university students. It was one of the most highly motivated groups I ever had the good fortune to be associated with. Out of a total of about ten participants, eight I believe made some major changes in their lives as a result of their group experience. By reading their letters, you may get an idea of their feelings during the afterglow period.

Dear Tom:

Thank you for the beautiful letter.

As you know, the very first thing I did when I got home was march upstairs and confront my father. I think he was relieved. We both cried and said we loved each other. After all that time, I had my father back again.

Of course, that didn't solve everything. The next week we had a big blow-up, father vs. the rest of us. Things have cooled down and now everyone is on speaking terms. At the moment I don't know what is going to happen but I do know my mother and father have talked things over. In spite of everything I feel my parents love each other. Both have the habit of blaming everything on the other. I've gone to each individually and had them admit that what has happened is not all one person's fault. Within the next little while, I'd like to sit them down face to face and have them admit this to each other.

For the past year and a half, I've been dating a grad. student. We'd decided to get married but hadn't told anyone about it yet. There was one big complication—religion. He's very staunch Roman Catholic and I'm a not very staunch Protestant. I thought I could swallow the religion. Well I can't and I won't. Our relationship has been very honest and open so he knows about my doubts. Last week, I finally had guts enough to tell him it's over. I feel a lot for him but I know it's not enough to carry me through a marriage—especially a marriage where I would have to convert to a religion I have deep-seated doubts about. I think he understands. Certainly there is no bittnerness on either side. Breaking the relationship off won't be easy but it is the only honest solution.

Here goes a "true confession." I think I've known all along our relationship wasn't going to work but I've been hanging on because I liked the security and was afraid I couldn't find anyone else. There I admitted it.

I'm still feeling the effects of the T-group and feel as if I'm walking on air. I suppose the most frustrating thing about coming back was my inability to convey the wonderful feeling to anyone. No one understands. Mary told you about the experience in the Varsity office. There we were, glowing with happiness, love, and warmth and trying to share our feelings—the reaction ranged from indifferent tolerance to real hostility. People kept scoffing, "It wasn't reality. You were play acting. You just imagined the closeness. It wasn't really there, etc. etc." Finally I just got up and walked out. I'm sorry but I can't do anything for people with closed minds. It's their loss, not mine. You're right, Tom, no one can take this experience away from me. Furthermore, I won't let them.

Things will never be the same because of the T-group experience. I'm capable of a great deal of love and now I know it. I did a great deal of living during those thirty-six hours and no one can tell me I was play acting. I came away with a new confidence in myself. The group cared about and felt for me. I told the group things about myself I'd been hiding from everyone and they responded with affection. Thank you, Tom, and thank you to the rest of the group. I love you all.

I feel relaxed. For the last year or so, I haven't yelled, screamed, slammed a door or stamped my foot. I told myself I was tough-skinned and I didn't let things bother me. Obviously they were. It isn't healthy to keep emotions bottled up the way I do. It's a problem I'll have to deal with.

I saw Jean last week. She's quitting her job and going to B.C. for the summer. Good for her. I was afraid of meeting people outside the group—afraid we'd be at loss for words. Well Jean and I babbled away for ages (typical females).

Conrad told his parents what he thought about them and they responded by being pleased with the change in him and the improvement in communication. He says he's amazed at how the T-group helped him. I'm glad.

Marianne is still very happy. I think the whole Varsity office thinks Marianne and I are both crazy. Well as I said before until they open their minds, it's their loss not ours.

Bill phoned last week and he's coming down to the Varsity office to see me Tuesday. I'm looking forward to seeing him. Imagine—spend thirty-six hours with a person and it's as if you've known them for a life time.

Well, Dr. Tom, I'll follow orders and take good care of myself. I wish you health and happiness. I can't promise I won't let strangers play games with me but I'll try. I hope we do run into each other sometime. That's something to look forward to.

Love,

Muriel

Dear Tom:

I wanted to say one other thing, that the weekend was the most fantastic experience I'd ever had; it really shattered me and wrecked me up for awhile but I really did learn an awful lot. For one thing, I don't feel so cynical about people—or so hostile.

But like I miss the experience—it feels like a drug: I want more and things out there don't look very good after that.

And then I really miss everybody—

Well, I can't say much after that. Hope you can believe what I wrote. It's such an exercise in futility, typing to define feelings so that they come out sincerely.

I hope you can read this anyway (Please excuse the mess), that it rings true.

And I hope I'll get to see you again sometime.

With affection,

Silvia

On the negative side, apart from feeling discouraged by "the scoffers" you may find your former friends dull and their conversation superficial. You may wish to quit your job and embark on a new career or a new life-style.

For the therapist, group weekends are extremely taxing both physically and mentally. He gets very little rest or sleep and the emotional demands on him are high. Sometimes two or three people in the group at any one time are extremely upset and require his attention. There is always the possibility of physical violence or major personality disintegration. A patient may not participate or constantly criticize the proceedings, and this acts like a dark cloud over the group. Then there is the whole problem of the marathon—will it click? To the therapist and his family, his absence from home one weekend every month is a major strain. They would like him to spend more time with them, his patients would like him to do more marathons.

# Summing Up

Because of the unique nature of the marathon's structure—its setting, time span, informality—it is a singular process. Naturally, it will be influenced by the theoretical orientation and leadership style of the group facilitator.

During the weekend all interactions evolve through three distinct, although overlapping, stages.

The major objectives of the beginning phase are
1) to get the participants acquainted with each other;
2) to get them thawed out;
3) to establish a flow of feelings toward and against some members;
4) to start developing trust in the process and the group leader.

The middle phase is characterized by a deepening of feelings and an increase of contact with others. There are several areas that group members may shy away from—for example, open expression of anger, sadness, negative feelings regarding their own or other people's bodies, and fear of death. They may require some help in getting into these areas.

The end phase is often the most difficult part of the weekend. It requires each individual to integrate into his life what he has learned during the marathon. Preferably, the experience will end on a positive, hopeful note, yet the participants must not leave so high that any little disappointment on their return to "civilization" will crush them.

# IX

# Consciousness
# Raising for Women
# and Men

Consciousness-raising groups are becoming an increasingly important facet of the group phenomenon in North America. Since they are very much concerned with personal growth, this book would be incomplete if I did not discuss them. Unfortunately, in a single chapter it is impossible to satisfy both the well-informed and uninformed reader. A glance ahead, therefore, will save you from reading things you already know or are not interested in.

Two sections, Looking Back in Anger and Women Power, deal with the sociocultural and historical factors that led to the present flourishing state of the Women's Liberation Movement. Under C.R. Groups, you will find a description of the formation, the day-to-day functioning, and the process of various types of C.R. groups. In C.R. Groups and Other Growth Groups, I examine the major similarities and differences between C.R. groups on one hand and T-groups, encounter groups, and therapy groups on the other.

In the course of working on this chapter I discovered to my horror that I was much more prejudiced against women than I realized. I do not believe that a few months spent reading the literature of the movement, talking to a great number of men and women, and attending C.R. groups has turned the tide of centuries. But it has made an impact on me. I hope this chapter reflects both my personal struggle as well as the struggles of thousands of men and women who wish to free themselves of the burdens of sexual stereotyping.

# Looking Back in Anger

During the last hundred years a few extraordinary women have raised their voices in anger against a social system which they claimed relegated them and all women to the status of an oppressed majority. Only during the last two decades, however, have women begun to organize and agitate collectively for true equality.

Both women and men are beginning to realize with increasing clarity that women have been discriminated against since history began. In the Old Testament Eve was pictured as physically, morally, and intellectually inferior to Adam, and among Jews and Christians this attitude became traditional. For example, Tertullian, one of the early Church Fathers (ca. A.D. 220), spoke of woman as a "temple built over a sewer. Women! you are the gateway of the devil . . . you should always go dressed in mourning and in rags."[1] *The Malleus Mallificorum,* written in 1484, and its detailed enumeration of tortures was used by the courts of the Inquisition for three hundred years to force women to confess

[1] PL.1, 1418b-19a. De Cultu feminarum, libri duo. I.1.

that they had had sexual relations with the devil and were witches. At Wertzberg nine hundred women were killed in one year; at Toulouse the devil must have been particularly busy because four hundred were executed in one day.

In orthodox synagogues women are usually relegated to sit either on the balcony or to the side or back of the main sanctuary behind some sort of a barrier. This is done so that men's thoughts will not stray from prayer and the study of the Torah. Even today, a daily prayer recited by the orthodox Jewish man is, Blessed art Thou, O Lord, Our God and King of the Universe, that Thou didst not create me a woman.

Our legal system treats women like chattels, reflecting the English common-law attitude to the effect that the husband and wife are as one—and that one is the husband. In some states a woman's income and property are still under the control of her husband. In most places a woman cannot be sterilized without her husband's consent and cannot have an abortion even with his consent. The prostitution laws discriminate too. Soliciting is an offense in thirty-four of the states of the union, but customers are subject to prosecution in only fourteen states and are hardly ever jailed.

Economically, the plight of women is appalling. The median income of white women, employed full time, is lower than that of white men employed full time. The income of black women is lower still. This, despite the fact that the median education of both groups of women is higher than that of their male counterparts!

Woman's role at the top of the labor force continues to be very small indeed. Only 3 percent of those working year round and full time earned $10,000 or more in 1968. Three percent as against 28 percent for men! It has taken forty years for American women to advance from 5 to 7 percent of the nation's physicians. They are 8 percent of the scientists, 3 percent of the lawyers. They constitute less than 1 percent of the engineers.[2]

Similarly, in the world of academy, the higher the rank, the lower the percentage of women. In a study of 188 major departments of sociology, Dr. Alice Rossi, a noted sociologist at Goucher College, found that women accounted for 30 percent of the doctoral candidates, 27 percent of the full-time instructors, 14 percent of the assistant professors, 9 percent of the associate professors, 4 percent of the full professors, and less than 1 percent of the departmental chairmen. At Columbia University, 25 percent of the doctorates go to women, but only 2 percent of the tenured faculty are women.[3]

Women are a majority of the population. They are also a majority in every racial and ethnic group. But they are almost invisible in government. There are no women on the Supreme Court, no women in the U.S. Senate, no women governors, no women mayors in the big cities.

This is merely one aspect of the discrimination against women that blights all parts of our society—economically, legally and socially, as well as politically.

## Women Power

The forerunners of today's feminists were the suffragists of a hundred years ago. By concentrating their energies on the question of the franchise, they lost sight of the single forceful argument for equality, as expounded in the Declaration of Independence and reinforced by the fight against

[2] *Women's Role in Contemporary Society:* The Report of the New York City Commission on Human Rights, Avon Books, 1972, New York p. 69.
[3] *Ibid,* p. 569.

slavery. After World War I came the "emancipation of women" and the right to vote. According to Connie Brown and Jane Seitz, "Somehow, what occurred was a terrible, cynical undercutting and buying off of the concepts of sexual, political and economic liberation, and their replacement by new, more versatile forms of servitude."[4]

During World War II, millions of women discovered that they could do a "man's job" and do it well. Yet, when the war was over the men returned to their former jobs, and the women were shunted back into their homes or relegated to lower-paying positions. Women suddenly realized that something was amiss. This growing undercurrent of dissatisfaction began to find expression in the writings of Simone de Beauvoir and Betty Friedan, who were followed by increasingly militant and activist spokesmen (spokespersons?), such as Germaine Greer and Kate Millett. Essentially, they said that women no longer wanted "to be supporting characters, stage hands, or applauding audiences for male achievements and men's dreams."[5] They began to rebel against being programmed to believe that they were inherently mentally and physically inferior to men. The task before them was how to reprogram centuries of sexist indoctrination and transform the New Woman into a person with the same rights and aspirations as men—all this without using yardsticks established by men to decide what is feminine and what is masculine.

The current Women's Liberation Movement, which aims to achieve these goals, was begun on a political level largely by alumnae of the civil-rights movement, campus movements, and the antiwar movement. After a while they initi-

---

[4] Robin Morgan, editor, *Sisterhood is Powerful*, Vintage Books, New York, 1970, p. 27.
[5] Muriel James, "The Down-Scripting of Women for 115 Generations," *Transactional Analysis Journal*, vol. 3, no 1, January 1973, p. 20.

ated the formation of women's caucuses within these organizations. Men's reactions ranged from polite derision to physical violence.

In 1966, the National Organization for Women (N.O.W.) was formed. It pledged to "bring women into full participation in the mainstream of American Society . . . exercising all the privileges and responsibilities thereof in truly equal partnership with men." N.O.W. is one of the very rare groups within the women's movement that allows men as members. It works within the system — lobbying legislators, writing reports, and forming committees. More militant organizations, such as W.I.T.C.H., see N.O.W. as a bourgeois feminist movement that does not reach out beyond its own class and race and that is satisfied with the established order of things. The radical groups see ecological destruction, the nuclear threat to our planet, racism, capitalism, and imperialism as outgrowths of the concept of male supremacy (which they refer to as sexism). They are bent on destroying that concept.

# Consciousness Raising

In 1966–1967 a number of radical women began to meet and talk about their personal problems in small groups. These meetings became known as "bitch sessions," "rap sessions," or "consciousness-raising (C.R.) groups." Some organizations in the movement utilized C.R. techniques only for a few months before moving into direct social action. Others remained primarily talk groups until such time as they were ready to break up. Still others developed along both lines.

C.R. groups are the heart and soul of the Women's Liberation Movement. They are formed either informally by a few friends getting together, inviting other friends to join them, and meeting in their respective homes, or within the framework of an established feminist organization or center—for example, the Princeton Women's Place, the Queens Women's Research and Resources Center, and the CUNY Women's Coalition. The great majority of C.R. groups are made up of women, although an increasing number are being formed now for men as well as for husbands and wives.

According to feminists, only a C.R. group composed entirely of women can perform its functions. Their reasoning seems cogent. With men present, some women may fall into their habitual patterns, roles, and games. They may abdicate leadership in the group to the men, be little-girlish or seductive, or use men as adversaries—enemies to be converted or wiped out. Since women traditionally have been isolated from one another (feminists refer to other women as their "sisters"), each woman has been made to feel her problems were unique. In other words, women's depressions have been interpreted as an expression of their neuroses instead of as the legitimate result of feelings of despair and uselessness that are induced by their status as appendages to their male associates, friends, lovers, and husbands. Where men's problems generally have been perceived as important—"business" problems, for example—women's difficulties usually have been taken much more lightly and brushed off as premenstrual tensions—"She's tired because she doesn't know how to organize her housework properly," or "She worries too much about the kids; she is overprotective, you know."

Wherever women and men go in our society they are forced to play roles. But because women have fewer opportunities just to be with other women, they also have had less opportunity to explore who they really are. In intimate and supportive C.R. groups women are now learning to be free and honest with each other. Here, often for the first time, a woman can voice her hopes and anxieties without being ridiculed. She frequently finds that others share her concerns. Indeed, it is one of the fundamental rules of C.R. groups that no participant interrupt, judge, or offer solutions to another. A woman may be questioned or asked to elaborate, but she will not be grilled as to the accuracy of her perceptions or the veracity of her facts. Members are encouraged to speak of their personal experiences rather than theorize or generalize; this has been called "giving testimony." For many women, the chance to speak about themselves without being challenged by a parent or other authority figure is a unique experience. It is quite liberating, often exhilarating.

Who are the women who join C.R. groups and how do they get there? The majority are middle class, white, and well educated. They span the spectrum from high school girls to middle-aged housewives to radical lesbians. They may first come to a Women's Place out of curiosity, or because a friend suggested it, or because something "clicked" in them. In the parlance of the movement, click refers to a sudden realization by a woman that she is not being treated as an equal by men—that she is a victim of sexism.

The women who run women's lib organizations are usually young, university trained, politically left-leaning activists. They resist coming on as experts, volunteer their services, and frequently live with like-minded women in small, urban communes. Their activities include organizing C.R. groups; offering courses for women in self-defense, plumbing, car repair; and funding various projects, such as interval houses for women with children whose husbands have left them, service information centers, health food co-ops, or women's publishing companies. There is hardly a campus or a city with more than 100,000 people that does not by now have some organization engaged in promoting women's liberation.

A typical first night of a C.R. group would see women of all ages sitting around in blocs of two or three, sipping coffee (a necessity at C.R. groups) and making small talk. After about twenty minutes the meeting begins. A few minutes will be spent on "who else is coming?" Then, having settled the problem of who is there and who is not, the person who initiated the meeting—not called a leader (the movement has a strong aversion to professional expertise when it comes to consciousness raising)—may say why she is there and tell a little about herself. She may explain what brought her into the movement, how long she has been in it, how she has benefited from it, and the like. Next, she will ask each participant to state why she is there and what she hopes to gain from the group. Following this some decision is made concerning general direction the group will follow.

The group's size at its inception is often twelve to fifteen; by the third or fourth session that number is whittled down to a comfortable eight to ten. Although a homogenous group—comprised of women of the same age and socioeconomic background—can get comfortable faster, heterogenous groups have the advantage of demonstrating convincingly how women's problems transcend age, employment category, and marital status. Heterogenous groups are thus more probing in nature.

Most groups meet for about two and a half hours once a week. In addition, some women's centers have C.R. and lesbian drop-in nights. Regular attendance is important, as is the confidentiality of all communications.

Some women will wish to stay emotionally uninvolved and are primarily interested in the study of the theory of women's liberation. If they are in the majority, the group may elect to spend one or several sessions on such subjects as Women in Literature; the Role of Women in the Family, the Professions and Society; Women and Sex; Rape; Abortion; the Black Woman; the Mexican-American Woman; and Psychiatry and Women. Other participants will be eager to explore their own personal lives in depth; they will probably opt for a nonstructured group and talk about such things as job discrimination; unsatisfactory marital relationships; sexual problems; and their feelings about their bodies, about men, money, menses, adolescence, and menopause.

Whichever route the group originally takes, the two begin to merge after a while. The cognitive group begins to talk feelings, and the experiential group starts to exchange books about various aspects of the movement and to invite guest speakers to talk on subjects that are of interest to them. Sooner or later all the participants start to analyze how their own background and society have molded them into what they are today. Once they realize the extent of their predicament, a shock of recognition and often sustained anger ensue. Years of suppressed bitterness surface and disrupt the lives of these women. Although statistics are not yet available, my personal impression is that about one-third to one-half of all married women who enter a C.R. group eventually separate from their husbands. Some of those who stay are self-admittedly hell to live with for many months. They often interpret every remark, gesture, or contact with a man in negative, often paranoid, fashion. If a man tries to be understanding, he is seen as patronizing; if he makes a decision—no matter how minor—without his wife, he is a bully; if he wishes to initiate sexual relations, he is called a sex-crazed animal with insatiable appetites.

Naturally, as the sessions progress, women will either hear or say things which may make them quite anxious or depressed. Several C.R. participants told me that, in such an instance, they would not consider seeking outside professional help. "The only place I can be that new person is at the center and I would not look for understanding outside of it," is a very common response. Others might consult a woman psychiatrist or psychologist, but only if she is thought to be free of sexist attitudes—for example Phyllis Chesler, author of *Women and Madness.* Therapists like Dr. Chesler will not try to foist existing standards of femininity and masculinity on a female patient, as nonliberated helpers might. Rather, they will help her find her own personality— even if it should turn out to be highlighted by characteristics that are often deemed more masculine than feminine.

Unfortunately, in my opinion, Dr. Chesler does a disservice to her cause by making exaggerated claims, and using psychoanalytic interpretations where it suits her. For example, she tells of a woman in Lansing, Michigan, who received shock therapy to stop her from having extramarital affairs because they upset her husband. Although I doubt the accuracy of this case history, I have no doubt at all that it is not representative of the mainstream of American psychiatric practice. To imply that this sort of thing happens often is mischievous in the extreme. Dr. Chesler feels that psychiatrists, obstetricians, and gynecologists reject the positive aspects of their ambivalence toward their mothers by learning to regard all women as disgusting and neurotic. In this way they gain control over both their forbidden love for mother and their fear of her. This seems to me so obviously farfetched that it makes analytical rebuttal superfluous.

Much time in both men's and women's C.R. groups is spent examining social stereotypes of the two sexes. In the male C.R. group which I attended we listed all the adjectives which we thought reflect how the average man perceives him-

self and his female counterpart. Here is the complete list
as it was written on the blackboard during our fourth session:

| Man | Woman |
|---|---|
| Aggressive | Unstable |
| Rational | Flighty |
| Paternal | Sexy |
| Authoritarian | Passive |
| Decisive | Submissive |
| Potent | Graceful |
| Successful | Delicate |
| Superior | Beautiful |
| Sophisticated | Poor driver |
| Strong | Impatient |
| Perseverance | Warm |
| Doesn't cry | Gentle |
| Adventurous | Cries a lot |
| Materialistic | Naïve |
| Diplomatic | Jealous |
| Persuasive | Catty |
| Competitive | Chatty |
| Athletic | Motherly |
| Loyal | Manipulative |
| Reliable | Sly |
| Just | Timid |
| Masculine | Irrational |
| Virile | Feminine |
| Intelligent | Superficial |
| Camaraderie | Martyr |
| | Moralistic |
| | Sensitive |
| | Artistic |
| | Weak |
| | Inattentive |
| | Sentimental |

No attempt was made to match a masculine quality against a feminine one. The assembled men simply threw out suggestions, and when the majority agreed that a given suggestion was a good descriptive phrase it was jotted down. It is evident from the list that women are seen as weaker than men, less rational, less reliable, and more emotional. Just about the only positive qualities from a male standpoint on the female side of the ledger were sensitivity, warmth, and beauty.

A C.R. group of women, meeting next door, were asked to engage in the same task. They ended up with virtually an indentical list. The only significant addition they made was to describe men as "always out for sex."

The men then decided to write down all the qualities we felt would be desirable in an ideal male and female. The list for the ideal male was as follows:

| | |
|---|---|
| Integrity | Courageous |
| Sensitive | Wise |
| Fair | Knowledgeable |
| Warm | Flexible |
| Sensuous | Resourceful |
| Sexy | Clean |
| Good judgment | Kind |
| Creative | Desire for contentment |

When we started to work on the ideal woman we discovered that every adjective or noun used to describe the ideal man also applied to her. This was quite a revelation.

The women once again ended up with the same list (somewhat shorter), and said that they did not even attempt to describe the ideal man since they realized right away that he would have to be the same as the ideal woman. So much for masculine and feminine traits.

Old ideas are, or course, difficult to change. Men cling to the status quo because who they are and what they are

doing is generally pretty close to what they were programmed to expect from life. Only when they are forced
by circumstances to examine their lives closely do they discover the stress and limitations of their masculine roles—
the price they have to pay for not showing feelings and for
striving to become successful.

Women are much more likely, either on their own or
under the gentle prodding of feminist literature or a friend,
to express a desire to change. Although they are rarely politically minded when they join the movement, they readily
support changes aimed at equality on the job and in the
home. But they become cautious when it comes to locating
the origins of discrimination in society or in seeking group
solutions to their problems. The greatest difficulty that
radical feminists encounter in converting new recruits to
their way of thinking is the new members' belief that individual solutions are possible. Most women at the present time
are not willing to follow the Marxist-Leninist line toward
a political revolution. They are primarily concerned with
personal growth and with making society more humane and
more liberal.

The post-C.R. woman usually falls into one of two distinct categories. She either remains in the movement, working in a social-action group such as a N.O.W. committee or
a distress center, or she returns to her former subculture
more aware, more integrated, but not calling "foul" every
minute of the day.

One woman who belonged to a C.R. group and is still
a strong advocate of women's liberation told me that she has
seen many women in the movement get stuck in the equivalent of the "terrible twos." She said, "When one of my sons
was two years old, he came downstairs to breakfast and said
no to his orange juice. Then he cried because he wanted it
so much. He felt that the only way he could make his own

choice was to say no." This woman felt that many of her sisters are doing just that. "Yet, without a no we don't have a yes. The woman who is told by her husband never to refuse him sexually can only comply; she can never say yes. Asserting the right to say no is a necessary first step. Some women confuse the right to say yes with the old compliance. A truly liberated woman can say yes or no to sex, she can be a mother, stay home, or go to work; she can do anything she wants to."

# C.R. Groups and Other Growth Groups

Most C.R. group participants resent established forms of growth experiences, such as encounter groups or group therapy. They generally avoid recognizing any similarities between what they are doing in C.R. groups and what is accomplished in growth groups. Yet C.R. groups work so well precisely because they share so many of the basic concepts and techniques of traditional therapy groups—for instance, size of the group, duration, frequency of meetings, stress on open and honest communication, discouragement of abstract discussions in favor of personally meaningful comments, and emotional support. Provided that the group does not stumble along leaderless or suffer too much change in its membership—which once again would apply to other groups discussed in this book—it will naturally move toward a close examination of each individual's present predicament, her family background, and her future aspirations. During this time many participants will learn that their most private terrors or the most personal sources of shame and embarrassment are common to many in the group. To be able to verbalize these fears, to learn that you are not the only one experiencing them, and to find that you are not rejected for having them is in itself of great therapeutic value. Intellectual and emotional insights follow which eventually lead to the formation of some plans for change and action.

Post-C.R. women, like successfully "encounterized" or "therapeuterized" women, report an increase in self-confidence, a growth in self-esteem, and a freeing of inhibitions. As one woman remarked, "Now I can get into a gut-level rapport very quickly with another woman who has been through the same experience." What sets them apart from more traditional groups is their apparent lack of an expert leader. I use the word "apparent" advisedly, since no matter how much the organizer or initiator of the first meeting will deny her expertise, the group looks to her for leadership, and she in turn offers suggestions as to how the group should function in the light of her experience. After a few sessions, internal leadership arises in the group, with some women becoming the natural pacesetters for the others. If the group were composed entirely of persons with no previous C.R. exposure (unless some members were sensitive to the needs of others and capable of channeling those needs into group decisions), the group would not survive. Consequently, the presence or absence of an expert in group leadership is simply an exercise in semantics.

The major difference between C.R. groups and other growth groups is that the former view women and men as victims of sexual-role stereotyping. C.R. groups are also convinced that our society requires radical restructuring in the direction of socialism. Since most women, at one time or another, have felt oppressed and exploited by men, and since most women are poorer than their husbands (even if both of them work), those who participate in C.R. groups are attracted by the ideologies of the political left. Unlike the psychotherapy patient, they are more likely to see their problems as socially, rather than individually, determined.

# Summing Up

The C.R. group, like T-groups and encounter groups, is designed to assist a healthy, normal individual to gain a greater awareness of herself or himself within the social context. With the help of C.R. groups many women and men are successfully breaking out of the caste system. Hopefully, although the transitional period will be a trying one, both sexes will arrive at a point of understanding. They will then regard themselves and respect each other as unique individuals with certain strengths and weaknesses rather than as masculine or feminine stereotypes.

# Questions You Have Always Wanted to Know the Answers to but Had No One to Ask

## X

*What's the Difference between a Psychologist and a Psychiatrist?*

*A psychologist* is a person who has taken a postgraduate degree, such as an M.A. or a Ph.D., in psychology. Psychology is an academic discipline like anthropology, archeology, and English literature. Its subject matter is the study of mental processes and behavior in animals and man. Some psychologists are research oriented, others teach, still others (clinical psychologists) specialize in psychotherapy. The training of a clinical psychologist typically consists of three years at a university to obtain a B.A., two years for an M.A., two years for a Ph.D., for a total of about seven to eight years. During this time he will have worked in social agencies and medical clinics and treated patients under supervision.

*A psychiatrist* is a medical doctor who has successfully

completed the requirements for additional training in this specialty. The psychiatrist is a specialist, as is a surgeon, pediatrician, or ophthalmologist. His training consists of two years of premedical school or its equivalent (B.A.), four years of medical school (M.D.), one year of internship, and four years of training in psychiatry (in the United States only three years are required and then two years in practice before the doctor is "board eligible"). Thus it takes a person at least eleven years to become a licensed practitioner of psychiatry.

Psychiatry, as opposed to psychology, is a medical science and deals with the origin, diagnosis, treatment, and prevention of mental and emotional disorders. In its purest form the locus of psychology is the healthy mind, that of psychiatry the diseased mind. Psychiatrists, as medical doctors, are qualified to prescribe drugs for their patients; psychologists are not.

Because psychotherapy is where the action is, psychiatrists, psychologists, social workers, clergymen, guidance counselors, and nurses have all moved into this field during the last two decades. Each group thinks that it can do a better job than the others, and there is a lot of hostility among them. But, in fact, there are good, competent people in each group—even among the nonprofessionals. The final choice is yours.

### Should Everyone Attend an Encounter Group?

Someone once said, "Group therapy is to make the sick well, encounter groups are to make the well better." Anyone who is not grossly disturbed can certainly benefit from a T-group or encounter group. I think though, it is very important not to push a person too hard to join a group. A husband or wife or friend who has just attended an encounter group may be so enthusiastic about it that he will, for the best of motives, want everyone to share his experience. His enthusiasm may produce an effect opposite to the one he desired and actually turn some people off.

Individuals who are highly defensive, rigid, and antagonistic to the human potential movement's general philosophy and aims will not gain much from attending a growth group. Men and women who have had major life problems in the past—if they were orphaned, have suffered from polio, or were incarcerated in a concentration camp, for example—and who have made a good adjustment to life are also best left alone. Their pain is too great to be adequately dealt with on one weekend.

With the above exceptions, I think that almost anyone would benefit from an encounter group and the world would be better if everyone attended.

### Is Nudity Part of All Encounter Groups?

The mass media have a way of focusing on the most controversial aspects of any new phenomenon—as growth groups were a few years back—and exaggerating it to the point of distortion. This is what has happened to nudity in groups.

At Esalen, participants often relax at night in the hot springs—in the buff. Elysium Institute and a few other centers in the United States state that clothes are optional. Paul Bindrim conducts nude marathons. Otherwise, encounter groups as a rule do not employ nudity—though you will find nudity where the group has access to warm water and where the leader has made it quite explicit at the start that this was part of the normal functioning of the group.

Nudity is definitely not practiced by T-groups or the average encounter group. When it does occur, it does not lead to sexual orgies. It leads, rather, to a freeing experience, which I think is most beneficial, especially for the uptight over-thirty generation.

## Should a Couple Attend the Same Group?

There are groups of couples only, which stress exploring the relationship between the two partners. It's O.K. for a couple to attend one jointly. But groups which consist of individual members are really worthwhile only for achieving personal goals.

Very few people can be totally honest in a group if their fiancé(e) or spouse is present. If your wife accompanies you, you may easily slip into one of your standard arguments and then either not talk about it in the group or talk about it and get hell for taking up the group's time with material that does not concern them. The other members want to know how you react to *them,* not your wife. Moreover, during the rest periods or after the conclusion of the session you may wish to speak to a few people who interest you. But with your wife beside you, you will feel obligated to spend time with her.

If you attend a group with someone you know, you will tend to stay aloof from the rest of the group and will not experience the loneliness and sense of separation from other people that is an essential feeling to have at the start. Loneliness accentuates all your self-doubts, and leads indirectly to a reappraisal of your personality. It is also good to have some time to yourself—time to look at the night sky, listen to the birds, and just be with your own thoughts.

Therefore, I suggest that you do not attend a group

with your marital partner unless the group is specially designed for couples.

### Should Friends Attend the Same Group?

No—for the same reasons that a couple should not attend the same group. There is, however, one other thing I would like to say about friends.

People once in a while tell me, "I see no reason for coming to group. I can have these kinds of conversations with my friends. We are very open and honest with each other." No matter how truthful a person is with his friends he is never totally truthful. Eric Berne's definition of a friend is an individual who plays the same games that you do. Put another way, a friend often has the same blind spots as you have and can no more help you with your shortcomings than he can help himself. Furthermore, your friends—as well as your family—have a vested interest in your remaining unchanged. They may tell you differently, but, in fact, if you begin to change, their relationship with you may be jeopardized. They may lose you, and they need you. So they resist any alterations in the status quo.

The conclusion is unavoidable: If you want to grow, you require an expert, not a friend.

### Will My Marriage be Affected by Joining a Group?

Neurotics marry neurotics. As you improve, you may help your spouse to straighten himself out. So if he or she has fewer hangups than you, then your new self-confidence, better sexual adjustment, and more direct communication will help to establish greater intimacy and joy in your marriage. This, however, is not always the case.

In some marriages, one partner can only appear to be coping as long as the other one is "sick." Also, there are families where one of the children is labeled as "sick." As long as this child acts strangely, the rest of the family can function quite well. Abolish the sick role and the true pathological forces emerge in the family. In such cases, it is imperative to get the other spouse or even the whole family involved in therapy.

Usually, it is a good idea for both spouses to participate in the same kind of a group. This helps each partner to appreciate what the other person is experiencing. For example, the husband who has been to an encounter group weekend will be able to calm his wife's fears about attending and be better able to understand her mood when she returns.

## Will My Job Suffer?

As a result of a T-group or encounter group, one's performance on the job rarely suffers; in fact, it often improves. On the other hand, weekly group therapy sessions may produce mood swings and periods of preoccupation in some members. This is usually the case with people who feel very hostile toward the group and are not able to discuss their hostility, or who are having pressure exerted on them by the group to take a step toward change but are unwilling to do so.

In the long run, any effort at personal growth may result in significant shifts of one's values and life goals. More specifically, if a man comes to identify with the encounter group ethic, he will likely desire to pursue an occupation which is more than just a means of earning a living. Thus, an executive with Consolidated Tools may

decide to quit his job and help build low-cost townhouses
or purchase a farm or make children's toys.


## Do Psychiatrists See Only Crazy People?

In the eighteenth century they did. Not so today. Yet
many people still think of psychiatrists in one of two
stereotyped ways. First is the jailer-psychiatrist who tries
to lock up as many patients as possible for as long as feasible
in an old, dilapidated lunatic asylum where indescribable
horrors await the poor devils. The other picture is of the
social-butterfly psychiatrist. He has a Viennese accent, sits
in a posh office, and sees only very rich and beautiful young
women whose only problem is how to seduce the psychiatrist.

Anyone who feels that he could benefit from talking over
his problems with a mental-health professional should feel
free to consult a psychiatrist, psychologist, or social worker.
No psychiatrist is in the least interested in certifying a
healthy person to a mental hospital. He gains nothing by
certifying a patient, and it involves a lot of paper work,
phone calls, and headaches. The mental hospitals themselves have very rigid criteria as to whom they accept as
patients. Moreover they try to discharge the patients they
have as quickly as possible. No one is dumped any more
in a large state hospital or a private little sanitarium and
then forgotten.

Sometimes I wish the second stereotype were true, but
it too is false. No self-respecting psychiatrist will accept
as a patient someone who does not require his services.
Many people need only a few visits to gain reassurance or
overcome their depression. And most women do not come
to a psychiatrist seeking a lover. The truth of the matter
is that the average psychiatrist looks and talks no differently

from the average obstetrician or stockbroker, and his clients span the whole spectrum of humanity.

## Should I Receive Therapy from a Person I Work with or Am Supervised By?

This should be avoided if at all possible. You cannot be quite open with a person who can get you fired or inhibit your academic progress. No matter how objective the therapist is, you will withhold information from him which may put you into a poor light.

A lot of people seek out a professional helper whom they have come to know as a student, employer, or friend. Avoid this at all costs. You are playing nasty, unconscious games, and you are creating a special relationship in which neither of you will be free agents. By selecting a person you know, you are automatically selecting a person who is the least likely to help you with your problems. You are really choosing a friend, and what I have said previously about friends applies here as well.

If, as a condition of employment, a therapist tells you that you need to be in therapy with him, try to escape this situation (unless the therapy you receive will be worth the risk you take in losing the position). It is preferable to refuse the therapy, but if you accept, make up your mind, and then stick to it. If you vacillate, you will neither benefit from the therapy nor keep your job.

## Can Anything I Say be Used against Me in Court?

According to the letter of the law, privileged communication exists only between a lawyer and his client. Clergymen have not been asked for hundreds of years to testify against their parishioners, but doctors, psychologists, social workers, and journalists have. In all English-speaking countries, there are a few precedents by which psychiatrists have escaped contempt-of-court charges and consequent imprisonment, because, in the opinion some judges, divulging what transpired in the therapeutic relationship would not have served the public good.

The problem of privileged communication arises most frequently in divorce actions, traffic accidents, and contested wills. You, as a patient or client, have a choice of instructing your therapist to testify or to refuse to testify. The control over your previous disclosures to him is always yours. However, if you ask him to keep all the exchanges between him and you secret and the judge instructs him to answer the opposing counsel's questions, unless your therapist wants to run the risk of being cited for contempt of court, he must answer. That is the law of the land. Fortunately, the law is often interpreted leniently. If the therapist holds fast and states clearly that under no circumstances will he divulge any information his patient has requested him to keep confidential, very few judges will rule against him.

Practically speaking, if you, as a client, have any concerns about having to go to court one day, ask your therapist how far he will go to protect the confidential nature of your disclosures. And even if you think you will never end up in court, it is prudent to ask him not to make any written notes about material which—in the wrong hands—could prove compromising to you. Advise him, too, as to what he may tell your relatives, friends, and employer about you.

It is extremely important to any health professional that he keep good and complete records about his patients. In order to avoid problems with the courts, some therapists do not write down information they consider potentially damaging to their clients, others keep two files, one "official" and another "private."

## How Can a Bunch of Neurotics Help Me?

When a therapist suggests to a patient that he might be helped with his problems if he joined a psychotherapy group, this question often pops out.

Other neurotics can help because even the most severely neurotic person has rational faculties and feelings which are healthy and appropriate. Moreover, their neuroses may hook into yours—masochists attract sadists, hysterics attract obsessive-compulsives, and psychopaths attract schizophrenics. By interacting in the group, your lifelong difficulties with people and your self-defeating patterns will be re-created, and you will be helped to recognize and correct them.

In the final analysis the only difference between the "neurotics" in the group and the people "out there" is that the group members at least realize that they have problems and are committed to solving them. Most of the "normals" lack even this minimal degree of insight.

## Who Should Be in Individual Therapy and Who in Group Therapy?

People who have deep intrapersonal problems and, consequently, need a lot of their therapist's time and attention benefit most from individual therapy. For problems of a sexual nature (such as impotence or frigidity), repeated bouts of depression, or phobias, single therapy also is best. Many patients, especially men, come to see a therapist because they feel too passive. Although this is a characterological problem of major magnitude, it does not lend itself well to conventional forms of individual therapy. A group, on the other hand, is able to make the life of a passive man so miserable that he either starts changing or quits. This is,

I think, preferable to staying in therapy for a few years and not gaining anything from it.

Group therapy is particularly effective for the large number of individuals who have problems with the opposite sex or engage in self-defeating behavior patterns, whatever their nature. Patients who are generally withdrawn and have difficulties relating are more suited to group than to individual therapy, although they have a tough time of it in either form of therapy.

There are still a lot of professionals who lack sufficient knowledge of group therapy to recommend it when it is clearly indicated. Then, too, there are a few therapists who place every person who consults them in a group. Make certain that the therapist who assesses you is familiar with all treatment modalities and does not allow his personal biases to influence his judgment.

## Can I Be in Individual and Group Therapy at the Same Time?

Therapists disagree on this question. Theoretically, a group patient makes the most progress by being only in group. This way whatever feelings develop in the group are taken back into the group. To provide a patient with an opportunity to vent his anger, for instance, against another group member in an individual session takes the edge off his anger at the next group meeting. Thus, instead of working out his problems with the person responsible for at least mobilizing them, he talks them out with his therapist. This not only does not allow the patient to experience the depth of his feelings, it also deprives the other patients in his group of a potentially important experience. Offering a patient both therapies, moreover, concurrently reinforces his neurotic need to be special. He does not experience fully the frustrations of his infantile strivings and never learns to master the fine balance between being self-reliant and inter-dependent.

I try to avoid giving individual therapy to patients who are in group therapy. I do make exceptions, however. There are patients who have so many problems or are so flooded with feelings that they need more therapeutic time than two and a half hours once a week. For people like this the only solution is to provide additional individual sessions. Patients who are undergoing a serious crisis in their lives also comprise a special category. It seems unfair to take up the group's time with domestic problems or school problems. Yet these are legitimate concerns with which patients need help. Still, when I undertake to give people both individual and group therapy, I attempt to limit individual therapy to as few hours as possible in order not to detract from the principal modality of treatment.

A variation of the individual-cum-group approach by one and the same therapist is to have therapist A see the patient individually while therapist B sees him in group. I know of no rationale for this idea except, perhaps, that therapist A only does individual therapy and therapist B only conducts groups. I think it is really counterproductive to be treated by two therapists. The patient can play one against the other, he can pretend to be receiving confusing advice, and he can sit on the fence and not make a commit-ment to either form of therapy.

### After I Terminate Group Therapy Will I Ever Need It Again?

The chances are very good that if you terminated by mutual consent you will never require group therapy again.

But there are no guarantees in life. Would you ask your plumber after he has fixed your sink if it would ever need fixing again?

The therapist has only helped you get on the right track. You must continue to work on yourself for a long time to come. If you continue to grow and to learn to stay in touch with your feelings, you will be able to stay out of therapy permanently.

### Are Groups Overemphasizing Emotions at the Expense of Reason?

Probably, but I see nothing wrong with that. We live in a society which until recently emphasized "keeping a stiff upper lip," and "minding your own business." Any open demonstration of feelings—especially in men—was regarded as weakness, boorishness, or a sure sign of insanity. Emotional women were called hysterical, and only foreigners raised their voices and gesticulated with their hands when they talked. Against this background, where repression of feelings and rationality were prized over everything else, a new stress on the emotions is necessary to redress the balance of forces.

True, we may be at a point where the pendulum has swung too far in the opposite direction. Certainly among many young people emotions run so high that it is virtually impossible to sit down with them and have a rational discourse. In the final analysis, it depends on where you are located on the rationality-emotionality continuum. If you are too emotional and you cry every time a person looks at you the wrong way, you have to develop better controls. If you are too much in your head, as most of us are, you need to learn to feel with your guts.

*Can Group Work Help Resolve the Problems of Our Society?*

To the extent that the encounter movement has already changed the approach of many conventional therapists, it is having far-reaching social effects in the area of psychotherapy. T-groups, which are widely used in industry, education, and government, have changed the lives of hundreds and thousands of people. Similarly, the participants in the workshops, seminars, and marathons of approximately two hundred growth centers all over the world have contributed to the personal growth of thousands of people. And encounter groups have been successfully used to overcome social-strife situations, such as student-faculty confrontations, racial and ethnic animosities, police-hippie antagonism, and employer-employee distrust.

The greatest promise of the growth groups is that they provide us with a means by which, for the first time in the history of mankind, a person need not label himself "sick" before he can receive competent help with his problems. Normal, coping individuals, by joining one of these groups, can learn how to become more open, trusting, and real. Such people stand a chance of becoming better fathers and mothers than their parents were and thus of interrupting the neurotic cycle of all past generations. This is a large goal, but it is not beyond our reach.

# The Many Ways to Grow

## XI

I started assembling material for this book about five years ago. Since then many changes have occurred in the world, in my own personal growth, and in my convictions as to how best to help people become connected. As I listened to hundreds of hours of taped group therapy sessions and read the recent publications in the field of growth groups, I began to experience a sense of frustration and dissatisfaction. On the tapes, again and again I heard people speak of wanting to get better who were unwilling to inconvenience themselves or to experience the pain which is so much a part of every journey of self-discovery.

I have little confidence in the standard therapeutic approaches—those unaffected by humanistic psychology— because they are based on a philosophy of "let's be rational." Experts in the helping professions are acting as if Freud had never existed: They are trying to talk people out of being neurotic or psychotic. The fundamental problems for the mental-health expert are how to reach the six-month-old, the four-year-old, or the ten-year-old in a forty-year-old, and how to reach and bring to consciousness his moments of crises which for some reason have been fixated in his mind and which still exert a powerfully negative influence on his life. One of the major contributions of the encounter group movement has been to attack both of these problems. Fritz Perls' saying to a person sitting quietly in the hot seat, "You are not ready to work, let somebody else come up," represents a revolution in client-therapist relations. A traditionalist would interpret the resistance, a Rogerian would empathize with the patient's difficulties, an existentialist might talk of how helpless the individual made him feel. Only an encounter leader would tell a person to fuck off and play his games somewhere else. Even though this attitude sounds arrogant and insensitive I have come to gradually encompass it.

Psychiatry, psychology, and social work are not like surgery where all you need is a written permission from a patient and you can put him to sleep, snip off his appendix, sew him up, and discharge him from the hospital five days later as cured. A person who wants to grow in a helping relationship requires a good understanding of what this entails and a high degree of motivation. People who lack these qualities are better off pursuing other means of growth.

The human potential movement's introduction of a variety of special techniques designed to produce quick involvement, greater spontaneity, and a direct assault on an individual's defense system replaces the intellectual, urbane, tactful approaches of traditional therapy. Many of the techniques, by being nonverbal and noninterpretive, dispense with intellectualizations and are more successful than past methods of reaching the irrational recesses of the mind.

To say this is by no means easy for me. I started practicing psychiatry along traditional Freudian lines. Like most of my colleagues I did insight-oriented, dynamic psychotherapy. I worked on dreams, slips of the tongue, and transference manifestations. Then I began conducting group therapy, and I noticed that whenever people were interacting with each other instead of playing psychiatrists to each other they showed and experienced strong feelings. When they did so they often made connections with events in the past which seemed significant.

A turning point in my professional life occurred when I was asked to co-lead a six-day laboratory in human relations run by York University. Here, for the first time, I sat with complete strangers, many of whom I would ordinarily avoid, and observed them and me going through constant mood changes and contradictory feelings until as time passed we drew closer and closer. I saw that in the right circumstances, when people learn to trust and feel secure, they can be truly beautiful. I am still awed by man's potential for unspeakable brutality on one hand and his ability to make a fellow man feel godlike on the other.

As a result of this and similar laboratory experiences I began to shift emphasis in my therapeutic work from archeological digging expeditions into the past to the explorations of here-and-now issues and feelings. I became very interested in encounter groups and acquired a wide repertoire of techniques which I applied also in individual and group psychotherapy. I suppose my style at that time—this was about two years ago—would best be described as existential, humanistic, and experiential.

During this period, but particularly on group weekends, I became aware of the tremendous amount of anger and hurt that most of us have buried deep in the cellars of our unconscious and that conventional methods are hardly ever able to uncover. I had seen many patients come near to letting some of this pain out and although I encouraged them to persist in their efforts, I did not know how to assist them to succeed in this process. And so, throughout the years, I have had to terminate therapy with a number of patients who were not markedly improved either by their criteria or my own. They may have learned how to communicate better; they were more self-confident; often their job and domestic situations were more fulfilling; but deep down their core remained unchanged. This was difficult for me to bear. I continued doing what I did because I was convinced that I was a good therapist (relative to the state of our knowledge) and many of my patients were without a doubt doing extremely well.

About a year ago some of my patients started talking to me about a new book, *The Primal Scream.* I read it and I was not at all impressed. The very subtitle "The Cure for Neurosis" was enough to turn me off. But gradually an ever-increasing number of patients asked for primal therapy. So I began to experiment with Janov's method, and what I saw and heard really cannot be put into words. I saw people literally regress to babies or infants crying for the things they never had—which is mostly mother and father love. And when they cried and screamed and contorted their bodies enough they started changing in a fundamental way. So I underwent some primal experiences myself under the guidance of competent professionals and changed my whole practice over to primal therapy.

I feel very happy about the work I am doing now. A number of patients who came to group because they liked the others in the group and because it was "interesting," were frightened by the intensity of the experience and have quit. I was sorry to see them leave. Yet, I am glad that they did because those who have remained and those who have come into therapy since are people who, although afraid, are willing to confront themselves.

So in a way, I have come full circle. I am again interested in early memories. But instead of having my patients talk about their past, I ask them to relive it with all the emotions which they repressed because the memories were too painful to remember. For people with deep-seated problems that seriously affect their daily lives, I think this is the best method we have available at this time.

I do not believe, however, that the approaches described here are the only ones by which a person can gain in maturity and happiness. Only last week I received a letter from a young couple who have moved from Toronto, two hundred miles north. They have rented a small cottage for fifty-five dollars a month and a store with a workshop in the back in a nearby town. The husband will be building furniture while his wife will make cushions, dried flowers, and baking goods. They write that they have never been happier in their lives and that their "heads are really together." I think these people have found for themselves a style of life which is truly satisfying and fulfilling. I believe an ever-increasing number of city dwellers will be following their example in the future.

A few years ago I treated a woman who was quite disturbed. Her progress in therapy was extremely slow, yet she depended on it to keep her going. I repeatedly pointed out to her that she was not getting anywhere. At the rate she was going perhaps by the age of sixty she would be straightened out. All this was of no avail. Then a friend suggested she join a transcendental meditation society. She did, and she started changing remarkably. Not that she gained any better insight into her problems but she became more at peace with herself and was able to change jobs and terminate therapy.

What I am trying to say is that there are many ways to grow. You can take a Japanese martial art like aikido and while strengthening your body you also learn to center yourself. T'ai chi ch'uan, Sufi, Arica Training, yoga, all involve bodily exercises in the service of raising one's consciousness. There is a revival of interest in Eastern religions such as Hinduism, Buddhism, and Zen as well as Hasidism, a Jewish mystical movement that originated in Poland in the eighteenth century.

Many of the concepts of these religious movements are as applicable today as they were when written. Perhaps even more so. For example, according to Hasidic texts, "the origin of the conflict which I experience between myself and others is to be found in the fact that too often I do not know what I feel, I do not say what I mean, and I do not do what I say."[1]

In the final analysis, each man has to find his own way. It is my sincere hope that these pages have been helpful to the reader in that respect.

> . . . We shall not cease from exploration
> And the end of all our exploring
> Will be to arrive where we started
> And know the place for the first time. . . .
>
> . . . What we call the beginning is often the end
> And to make an end is to make a beginning.
> The end is where we start from. . . .
>
> —T. S. ELIOT, *Little Gidding, Four Quartets*

[1] Sheldon Kopp, *Guru,* Science & Behavior Books, Palo Alto, Calif., p. 41.

# Appendix I:

# Guidelines
# for Group Members

There are a few basic rules you should subscribe to when you join group. The following have been found helpful by my patients in the past.

1) The group process depends on the participants' openness and honesty. It is, therefore, essential that everything that transpires be kept strictly confidential. If you wish to discuss, with a close friend, what has happened, please talk about your reactions to person X or Y or speak in generalities. Do not mention even first names or other identifying information about group members, e.g., "this young actress who was on T.V. last night."

2) You may do and say whatever you like as long as you don't physically hurt someone in the group or aren't destructive to the furnishings.

3) There is to be no smoking during group. People usually light up when they are tense. We want to get at the root of

the tension, not cover it up. It is also strongly suggested that no tranquilizers, aspirin, alcohol, etc., be taken immediately preceding group. If you have a headache—bring it to group!

4) If you are going to be absent or late, please let us know. Should you miss three sessions in any three-month period, without notification: consider your therapy terminated.

5) If for any reason you wish to terminate therapy, please come to group and tell them about it face to face. No other form of ending group will be accepted.

In response to, "How to get the most out of group?" here are some general suggestions that may help you.

1) No matter how hard you may find it; *participate.* You cannot make progress unless you get involved and allow yourself to experience your true feelings and to react to others in the group. Question, challenge, say what you feel. Try to be as open and honest with yourself and others as you possibly can.

2) Make the group part of your life. In other words, don't think of group as something that happens on Monday between four and six o'clock and then forget about it until next Monday. After the group, think over what happened. What emotions did you feel when you talked about your brother? Why did you tell Y to leave Z alone? You may feel depressed or elated after group. Try to figure out why you should be feeling this way. Discuss it the next week.

3) If you wish to meet with group members outside of therapy, you may do so. But because you are in group, you will be expected to tell the group about it. Do not ask group members to keep a confidence outside of group. If you cannot talk about something to all the members, this is a good reason for bringing it up in the group.

4) You are not in group to be tactful or popular. Be yourself whatever that entails. Show the group all sides of your personality.

5) Don't wait for a long pause before you start talking or getting into your feelings. Make your own openings. Similarly, if you feel bored and you think that the person who holds the floor is going nowhere, *interrupt!*

6) This is *your* group and *your* therapy. If it is not moving in the direction you would like it to move, express your dissatisfactions. If at any one point you think a particular technique, e.g., psychodrama, would be helpful to another member, suggest it.

7) If you ever have a choice between saying something, e.g. "I feel sorry for you," or communicating these same thoughts or feelings through an action, *DO IT!* e.g., move over and put your arms around this person. When you do this be aware of your needs as opposed to the needs of the other person. Are you saying or doing something to fulfill your needs or his needs?

8) Do not ask theoretical questions, e.g., "Are most alcoholics orally fixated?" Rather, make a personal statement. Also, address others in the group directly: don't say, "Some people here don't like me." Who doesn't like you? Why don't they care for you, etc.?

9) Try to move into areas that are anxiety provoking both in and outside the group. If, for example, there is a person in the group you feel intimidated by, confront that person. If you have doubts about your femininity, get into that. Growth can only occur by going beyond the limits you have set for yourself in the past.

10) Experiment in and outside the group with new forms of behavior. Unless you start to act differently and to take some risks, you will not change!

# Primals

1) If you want to work on an incident in the present or past that has a lot of feeling attached to it or on a definite emotion, explain briefly what you feel, then get into it. You may, if you so desire, ask a specific person in the group or more than one person to come and help you with your feelings. Do not worry about looking silly, losing control, going mad, etc. Just do it and the group will look after you.

2) Allow yourself to react emotionally to what is happening. You can help guide another person by keeping him on a regressive track, not allowing him to intellectualize, watching his body and responding to its signals, and protecting him from harming himself or others.

3) If you are not "on" but begin to experience feelings, do not bottle them up. Ask some member of the group to come to your aid, lie down wherever it is convenient and go with your feelings.

# Appendix **11**:

# Resource Guide

On the following pages I have listed books, journals, tapes, records, poems, growth centers, etc., which will give you further information. For example, if you wish to know more about gestalt, Fritz Perl's *Gestalt Therapy Verbatim* might be a good book to start with. Having read that you may wish to read his more theoretical *Gestalt Therapy* or his biographical *In and Out the Garbage Pail*. From there you may obtain some of his gestalt training tapes and films, or you may become involved in gestalt workshops as a participant and eventually undergo training at a gestalt institute and become a gestalt therapist.

Although I have tried to be eclectic and cover the whole spectrum of orthodox analytic to occult transpersonal orientations, I have also tried to indicate my personal preferences. I hope that this attitude, rather than being a hindrance will be of help both to the layman and the informed professional.

# Journals/Newsletters

*Psychology Today*
Communications Research Machines, Inc.
Carmel Valley Rd., Del Mar, Calif. 92014

This is a monthly magazine about psychology, society, and human behavior. It is beautifully laid out and never fails to have at least a few articles that are genuinely thought provoking. Typical topics include:

"Whole Soul Catalogue of Humanist Psychology and Its Technology of Personal Growth"
"TV Violence and Child Aggression"
"The Feel Wheel, a game"
"Freud's Friend, *Theodor Reik:* A Conversation"
"Talks with: Piaget, Arthur Koestler, Margaret Mead, Herbert Marcuse"
"The Many Masks of the Healthy Man"

*Behavior Today*
Box 2993, Boulder, Colo. 80302

A weekly, usually a four-page newsletter, crammed with items concerning the social science scene. Up-to-date reports on legislation, political changes affecting large organizations, recent research findings and upcoming meetings. Very helpful for those interested in seeking private or government grants.

*The Journal of Humanistic Psychology*
584 Page Street
San Francisco, Calif. 94117

Semiannual publication of the Association of Humanistic Psychology. Topics of special interest are authenticity, encounter, self-actualization, search for meaning, creativity, and personal growth. Typical issues dealt with:

"Humanistic Psychology and the Philosophy of Science"

"The Humanistic Ethic"
"Creativity and Psychopathology: A Theoretical Model"
"Alfred Adler and Humanistic Psychology"
"A Humanistic Psychology"
"A Humanistic Program for Change in a Large City School System"
"Levels of Existence: An Open System Theory of Values"

*Newsletter*
Association for Humanistic Psychology
416 Hoffman St.
San Francisco, Calif. 94114

An informed monthly publication dealing with who is doing what in the Human Potential Movement. Received with your membership in A.H.P.

*The Group Leader's Workshop Newsletter*
Explorations Institute
P.O. Box 1254, Berkeley, Calif. 94701

A monthly newsletter focusing on techniques and concepts of groups, particularly encounter groups. Some representative articles:
"Massage Workshops"
"Encounter Group Casualties"
"Ethics and Encounter Groups"
"Team Building"
"Reports from A.P.A. Conventions"
"Psychodrama and Its Diverse Uses"
"Guided Imagery"

*Society* (formerly *Transaction*)
Box A, Rutgers University
New Brunswick, N.J. 08903

A social science journal with articles by sociologists, psychologists, pyschiatrists, etc. Some of the typical subjects dealt with:

"Swinging in Wedlock"
"Death of the American Dream House"
"Carnivals, Road Shows, and Freaks"
"Pathology of Imprisonment"
"Israel and Its Third World Jews"
"Police as Folk Heroes"

*The Journal of Trans-Personal Psychology*
P.O. Box 4437
Stanford, Calif. 94305

Published semiannually, it is concerned with metaneeds, peak experiences, mystical experiences, transcendance of the self, cosmic awareness, and related concepts. Some representative articles:

"Baba Ram Dass lecture at the Menninger Foundation I & II"
"The Zen of Hubert Benoit"
"Meditation as metatherapy: Hypotheses toward a proposed fifth state of consciousness"
"On the meaning of transpersonal: Some metaphysical perspectives"
"Voluntary control of internal states: Psychological and physiological"

*Transactional Analysis Journal*
3155 College Avenue
Berkeley, Calif. 94705

Official journal of the International Transactional Analysis Association. Some of the articles follow Eric Berne's wit, as, eg., "Sleepy, Spunky and Spooky." Others get pretty convoluted, as, eg., "Second Order Structure of the Parent."

*The Journal of Applied Behavioral Science*
1201 Sixteenth St. N.W., Washington, D.C. 20036

Publication of the NTL Institute which runs a wide variety of T-groups, training of trainer programs, community, government and interracial groups. Representative articles:

"Leadership styles in Task-Oriented Committees"
"Sensitivity Training for Staff in an Institution for Adolescent Offenders"
"Analysis of the Thematic Structure of T-groups"
"Humanism and the Training of Applied Behavioral Scientists"

*NTL Institute News and Reports*
1201 Sixteenth St. N.W., Washington, D.C. 20036

Official publication of the NTL Institute for Applied and Behavioral Science. Concerned with T-groups, O.D. (Organizational Development), and research in groups.

*The International Journal of Group Psychotherapy*
239 Park Avenue South, New York, N.Y. 10003

Published quarterly, this is a stodgy, unimaginative, largely psychoanalytically oriented journal with articles like:

"In Tribute to S. R. Slavson"
"Analytic Supervision in Group Psychotherapy"
"Multitransferences and Divarications in Group Therapy"

*The American Journal of Group Psychotherapy*
1790 Broadway, New York, N.Y. 10019

A monthly publication of the American Group Psychotherapy Association. It is valuable while you are studying to become a group worker. After reading it for three or four years you will find it extremely repetitious.

*The American Journal of Psychiatry*
1700 Eighteenth St. N.W., Washington, D.C. 20009

The December 1969, vol. 126, no. 6 issue deals with groups from a largely psychoanalytic and critical standpoint. For a more balanced view read "Task Force Report #1 — Encounter Groups and Psychiatry," also published by the American Psychiatric Association, April 1970.

*Canada's Mental Health*
Mental Health Division
Dept. of National Health and Welfare
Ottawa, Ont. Canada

Vol. XIX, no. 5, September–October 1971 issue is dedicated to the human relations phenomenon. It provides an excellent overview of the subject, some historical notes, as well as an assessment of the present status of encounter groups in Canada.

# The Human Potential Movement

Severin Peterson
*A Catalogue of the Ways People Grow*
Ballantine Books, New York, 1971

As the title implies, this book is a handy reference guide to self-actualization disciplines. It covers everything from aikido to ESP to tarot and Zen. Some of the chapters are quite excellent and others are too far out for my taste.

Rasa Gustaitis
*Turning On*
The Macmillan Co., New York, 1969

Jane Howard
*Please Touch*
McGraw-Hill Book Co., New York, 1970

Both of these books were written by lady reporters who traveled across the United States learning about the various growth centers, NTL labs, Synanon, etc. Gustaitis is more personal in her account, while Howard ranges over a larger spectrum of groups. They are good books if you want to get the feel for the movement.

# Humanistic Psychology

A. H. Maslow
*Toward a Psychology of Being*
Van Nostrand Reinhold Co., New York, 1968

One of the theoretical foundation texts for the Human Potential Movement. A background in ego psychology and existentialism would be helpful to the reader who ventures into this book.

Clark Moustakas
*Personal Growth: The Struggle for Identity and Human Values*
Howard Doyle, 1969

C. R. Rogers & R. Stevens
*Person to Person: The Problem of Being Human*
Real People Press, Lafayette, Calif. 1967

C. R. Rogers
*On Becoming a Person*
Houghton Mifflin, Boston, Mass. 02107

J. F. Bugental
*Challenges of Humanistic Psychology*
McGraw-Hill Book Co., New York, 1967

Sidney M. Jourard
*The Transparent Self,* 2nd ed.
Van Nostrand Reinhold Co., New York, 1972

All the above listed books make important contributions to the study of humanistic psychology. If you have the time, read them all. If not, start with Rogers and Jourard.

# The New Therapies

Frederick S. Perls
*Gestalt Therapy Verbatim*
Real People Press, Lafayette, Calif., 1969

Here the originator and developer of gestalt therapy gives some clear explanations of the basic ideas underlying his approach. This is followed by verbatim transcripts of "complete" therapy sessions with explanatory comments.

The Fritz enthusiast will also enjoy reading his autobiography, *In and Out the Garbage Pail.*

Joen Fagan and Irma Lee Shepherd (ed.)
*Gestalt Therapy Now—Theory / Techniques / Applications*
Harper and Row, Publishers, New York, 1970

This book offers a wide sampling of theoretical papers, techniques, and applications by Fritz and Laura Perls, Claudio Naranjo, Erving Polster, and other well-known therapists and teachers. It attempts to bring gestalt therapy into historical focus. The book is well written and easy to read. Recommended for the novice as well as the seasoned psychotherapist.

Frederick Perls, Ralph F. Hefferline, and Paul Goodman
*Gestalt Therapy*
A Delta Book, Dell Publishing Co., Inc., New York, 1951

This is essentially the theoretical foundation of gestalt therapy. It is heavy reading but a must for those who want to go beyond the two-chair technique.

Eric Berne
*Games People Play*
Grove Press, Inc., 1964

The book was designed to be a sequel to Berne's *Transactional Analysis in Psychotherapy.* It became an instant best-seller and made T.A. popular. It is a fun book. Furthermore, it makes sense.

Muriel James and Dorothy Jongeward
*Born To Win — Transactional Analysis with Gestalt Experiments*
Addison-Wesley Publishing Co., Reading, Mass., 1971

Primarily concerned with transactional analysis theory and its application to the daily life of the average person.

Albert Pesso
*Movement in Psychology (Psychomotor Techniques and Training)*
New York University Press, 1969

This is somewhat similar to bioenergetics except that it involves body movement in relationship to self and others. Pesso unfortunately invents many new terms to explain what he is doing. This tends to confuse the reader. A good book for those interested in nonverbal approaches to the body.

Alexander Lowen, M.D.
*The Betrayal of the Body*
Collier Books, The Macmillan Co., Toronto, 1967

Dr. Lowen explains the basic concepts and techniques of bioenergetics in this easily readable book. His approach is essentially reaching the mind through the body instead of the other way around as most therapists do.

J. L. Moreno
*Psychodrama,* Vols. I, II, & III
Beacon House Press, New York, 1959

The founder of psychodrama describes his approach in detail illustrating his concepts with the use of case studies.

Samuel Kahn
*Psychodrama Explained*
Philosophical Library, New York, 1964

If you don't want to read Moreno's three volumes, here is a little book that deals clearly and succinctly with the theory, language, and practice of psychodrama.

Arthur Janov, Ph.D.
*The Primal Scream*
G. P. Putnam's Sons, New York, 1970

*The Anatomy of Mental Illness—The Scientific Basis of Primal Therapy*
G. P. Putnam's Sons, New York, 1971

*The Primal Revolution*
Simon & Schuster, New York, 1972

Janov's primal therapy is a theoretical integration of orthodox psychoanalysis, bioenergetics and gestalt therapy. His claim for having discovered "the cure for neurosis" and his attempt to discredit other therapists—even those doing primal therapy unless they were trained by him— have created needless hostility toward him by other professional helpers. Personally, I believe that primal therapy is by far the best and fastest road to self-change of all the methods available at the present time and will prove increasingly beneficial.

# Self-Awareness Techniques

William C. Schutz
*Joy (Expanding Human Awareness)*
Grove Press, Inc., New York, 1967

The book that popularized Esalen. Many methods for nonverbal communication, such as breaking in and out of the circle, fantasy trips, gestalt techniques, etc., are vividly described. A good first book for anyone contemplating getting into a here-and-now-oriented group.

Bernard Gunther
*Sense Relaxation—Below Your Mind*

This is a beautifully produced book with some really fine photographs. They help the reader follow many of the sensory awakening exercises described in the book. Highly recommended for couples who like to touch or who have forgotten how.

Gorden Inkeles and Murray Todris
*The Art of Sensual Massage*
Straight Arrow Books, San Francisco, 1972

In stunning pictorial form, this book will help the absolute beginner develop good massaging techniques. It is easy to follow—just get some oil and try it.

John O. Stevens
*Awareness: Exploring, Experimenting, Experiencing*
Real People Press, Lafayette, Calif., 1971

Most of the book consists of over one hundred experiments designed to help you explore your awareness and your relationship with others. Especially recommended for group leaders who wish to learn more techniques.

Herbert A. Otto
*Group Methods to Actualize Human Potential—A Handbook*
The Holistic Press, Beverly Hills, Calif., 1970

Yet another book on techniques. It is strong on fantasy e.g., "The Minerva Experience" and "The Death in Life Experience." The author also offers many ideas on having group parties with such themes as "the joy of being a child," "the joy of being a winner," "the joy of living your fantasies," etc. His constant emphasis on the positive and little homilies such as "Can we have a great paradise without if we do not first explore the paradise within" are irritating to me.

# Text on Group Therapy (primarily for professionals)

Hendrik M. Ruitenbeek (ed.)
*Group Therapy Today—Styles, Methods and Techniques*
Atherton Press, Inc., New York, 1969

This book offers a good review of the different approaches to group therapy by such people as Freud, Pratt, Adler, Slavson, Horney, and Sullivan. It has a few rather esoteric chapters—e.g., "Response of Married Couples Included in a Group of Single Patients" and "Some Comments on Transference when the Group Therapist is Negro"—but it also has some excellent chapters on recent trends—bio-energetics, art therapy, the marathon group.

Gerard Egan
*Encounter—Group Processes for International Growth*
Brooks/Cole Publishing Co., Belmont, Calif., 1970

This is the best theoretical exposition of the interpersonal dynamics of encounter groups that I know of. Valuable chapters on contracts, goals, leadership, and confrontation.

Milton M. Berger, M.D. (ed.)
*Videotape Techniques in Psychiatric Training and Treatment*
Brunner/Mazel, Inc., New York, N.Y., 1970

This is the first comprehensive presentation of every aspect of videotape in psychiatry. It covers videotape in psychiatric training and supervision, in hospitals and private offices, for individual, family, and group therapy. It is solid, informative, but rather dull.

S. H. Foulkes & E. J. Anthony
*Group Psychotherapy—The Psychoanalytic Approach*
Penguin Books Ltd., Baltimore, Maryland, 1957, 2nd ed. 1965

Two pioneers of the analytic approach to group therapy address their remarks to specialists in the field. This should be a basic text even for nonanalytically oriented therapists. Also includes a chapter on children and adolescents in group psychotherapy.

Irvin D. Yalom
*The Theory and Practice of Group Psychotherapy*
Basic Books, Inc., New York, 1970

Dr. Yalom deals with the role and technique of the therapist, the selection of patients, various stages of therapy, problem patients, etc. If you wanted to read but one book on group therapy, this is the one I would recommend.

# T-groups and Organizational Development

L. Bradford, J. Gibb, & K. Benne
*T-group Theory and Laboratory Method*
Wiley Co., New York, 1964

The classic textbook on the subject. Scholarly and thorough. It should be in your library but makes dull reading.

E. Schein & W. Bennis
*Personal and Organizational Change through Group Methods*
Wiley Co., New York, 1965

More attuned to working with organizational systems than the above. Recommended, if you're interested in organizations.

J. William Pfeiffer & John E. Jones
*A Handbook of Structured Experiences for Human Relations Training*, Vols. I, II & III.
University Associates Press, Iowa City, Iowa, 1969

These little books are a practical source of "structured experiences" which come in handy when you are designing your next lab. They are full of questionnaires, guides, charts, and worksheets. In other words, there is a great stress on pencil and paper methods as opposed to open encounter.

# Sex and Marriage

Dr. George R. Bach & Peter Wyden
*The Intimate Enemy: How to Fight Fair in Love and Marriage*
Avon Books, New York, 1968

This book may be of help to couples who bottle up their resentments.

Fred Belliveau & Lin Richter
*Understanding Human Sexual Inadequacy*
A Bantam Book, Little, Brown and Co., 1970

This is a clear and simple explanation of the work of Masters and Johnson.

*The Sensuous Woman by "J"*
Dell Publishing Co., Inc., New York, 1969

This is a male chauvinist's dream come true. At the same time it does offer some novel approaches to sexual joy and renews your interest in experimenting instead of doing the same old thing over and over again.

Alexander Lowen, M.D.
*Love and Orgasm*
Signet Books, The New American Library, Inc., New York, 1967

Based on Lowen's theories of bioenergetics, which are an updated version of Reich's orgasm concepts, it analyzes the connection between sexual functioning and personality.

Everett Shostrom and James Kavanaugh
*Between Man & Woman: The Dynamics of Intersexual Relationships*
Nash Publishing, Los Angeles, 1971

The authors examine the artificial roles that marriage partners tend to assume. They treat extensively the fulfilling and growth-producing relationship between a man and a woman, which they call "rhythmic."

# Thought Provoking

Charles Hampden-Turner
*Radical Man*
Schenkman Publishing Co., Cambridge, Mass., 1970

The author offers a model of psychosocial development, which he then applies to various social and political problems. The chapters on "Conservative and Radical Issues and Rebellion" and "Growth and Repression in Training Groups" are extraordinarily well written and pertinent to an understanding of the group phenomenon.

Sheldon B. Kopp
*Guru: Metaphors from a Psychotherapist*
Science and Behaviour Books, Inc., Palo Alto, Calif., 1971

This is a profound and beautiful book. Kopp distills the wisdom of gurus from many times and settings—from the shamans to priests to Zaddiks of Hasidism to the psychoanalysts and the humanistic therapists. One of those rare books that you finish feeling you would like to be friends with the author.

Alan W. Watts
*The Wisdom of Insecurity: A Message for the Age of Anxiety*
Pantheon Books, New York, 1949

Herman Hesse
*Siddhartha*
New Directions, New York, 1959

All of Hesse's books are worthwhile reading, but this novel is especially notable for its blend of depth psychology and Indian mysticism.

# Growth Centers and Other Training Facilities

For a fairly complete list of growth centers write the Association for Humanistic Psychology, 584 Page Street San Francisco, Calif. 94117.

In order to keep abreast of the most recent trends in personal growth approaches, get on the mailing lists of at least a few of the larger centers such as:

Esalen Institute
1776 Union Street
San Francisco, Calif. 94123

Center for the Whole Person, Inc.
1633 Race Street
Philadelphia, Pa. 19103

Oasis: Midwest Center for Human Potential
1439 S. Michigan Avenue
Chicago, Ill. 60605

Associates for Human Resources, Inc.
P.O. Box 727
Concord, Mass. 01742

Synergia
P.O. Box 1685, Sta. B.
Montreal 110, Quebec, Canada

The Gestalt Institute of Canada
P.O. Box 39
Lake Cowichan, B.C., Canada

Institute for Advanced Study in Rational Psychotherapy
Albert Ellis, Ph.D., Director
45 East 65th Street
New York, N.Y. 10021

NTL Institute for Applied Behavioral Science
1201 Sixteenth Street, N.W.
Washington, D.C. 20036

Rocky Mountain Behavioral Institute
12086 W. Green Mountain Drive
Denver, Colo. 80228

For those interested in nude encounters write:

Paul Bindrim Associates
2000 Cantata Drive
Los Angeles, Calif. 90028

Elysium Institute
5436 Fernwood Avenue
Los Angeles, Calif. 90027

Meditation-oriented centers:

Blue Mountain Center of Meditation (Hindu)
P.O. Box 381
Berkeley, Calif. 94701

Dramond Sangha
Koko An
2119 Kalva Way
Honolulu, Hi. 96822

"Yoga Life International"
Sivananda Yoga Vedanta Center
5178 St. Lawrence Blvd.
Montreal, Que., Canada

# University Affiliated Humanistic Psychology Programs

The Humanistic Psychology Institute

H.P.I. has been working closely with the Sonoma State College, Department of Psychology. For more details and other related courses write to A.H.P., which will also give you a complete listing of departments of psychology offering humanistic psychology courses.

Center for Applied Social Science
Boston University
270 Bay State Road
Boston, Mass. 02215

United States International University
The School of Human Behavior
8655 Pomerado Road
San Diego, California 92128

New York University
School of Continuing Education
100 Washington Square East
New York, New York 10003

The above centers offer various courses leading to B.A., M.A., and Ph.D. degrees in humanistic psychology.

University of Waterloo
Waterloo, Ontario

The Department of Psychology is offering a graduate program in human relations studies leading to the M.A. Sc. or Ph.D. degrees.

E.G.O. Programme
The Centre for Continuing Education
York University
4700 Keele Street
Toronto (Downsview), Ontario

Nondegree, nondiploma-granting workshops and seminars in encounter, gestalt, bioenergetics, transactional analysis, psychodrama, etc.

## Information Retrieval Sources

National Referral Center for Science and Technology
Library of Congress
Washington, D.C. 20540

Write for free advice on where and how to obtain information on specific topics.

Behavior Today
Del Mar, Calif. 92014

By special arrangement with Smithsonian Science Information Exchange, Inc., B.T. readers can order abstracts of all current research on file at S.S.I.E. Information includes finding source, principal investigators, and project descriptions.

## Tapes, Open Reels, and Cassettes

Recordings of past Esalen programs, highlights of past A.H.P. meetings, as well as hundreds of recordings of Abraham Maslow, Carl Rogers, William Schutz, Frederick Perls, Virgina Satir, John C. Lilly, Baba Ram Dass, R. D. Laing, Harvey Cox, etc., are available by writing to:

Big Sur Recordings
117 Mitchell Blvd.
San Rafael, Calif. 94903

## Films

The work of Frederick S. Perls, Alexander Lowen, Carl Rogers, Albert Ellis, Rollo May, and others is available from

Psychological Films
205 West Twentieth Street
Santa Ana, Calif. 92706

Association for Humanistic Psychology
416 Hoffman Street
San Francisco, Calif. 94114

Tapes and films on Paul Bindrim, Albert Ellis, Eric Berne, Alexander Lowen, etc., may also be obtained from their respective organizations.

Bell and Howell
Human Development Institute
20 Executive Park West
N.E. Atlanta, Georgia 30329

Multimedia programs to enhance human potential. Subjects include encounter tapes for personal growth, single adults, black/white groups, employees, and team development.

# Consciousness Raising for Women and Men

Simone de Beauvoir
*The Second Sex*
Alfred A. Knopf, Inc., New York, 1953

The first truly feminist book in the modern tradition. The position of women is examined from such varied viewpoints as biological, historical, psychological, literary, and religious. It is a work of great scholarship and little vitriol. In this respect the book differs markedly from some of the more recent publications on the same subject.

Germaine Greer
*The Female Eunuch*
Granada Publishing, London, Eng., 1971

"The characteristics [in women] that are praised and rewarded are those of the castrate: timidity, plumpness, languor, delicacy and preciosity." (p. 15) Her bitter and angry attack on the whole system of sex assumptions is must reading for anyone who desires a better understanding of the forces that are going to shape our future.

Betty Friedan
*The Feminine Mystique*
Dell, New York, 1963
and
Kate Millett
*Sexual Politics*
Doubleday & Co., Garden City, New York, 1970

Essentially, Betty Friedan writes in the tradition of Simone de Bauvoir, Kate Millett in the tradition of Germaine Greer. Ti-Grace Atkinson in the April 1973 issue of *Majority Report,* a New York feminist newspaper, attacks Betty as having sold out to the establishment and desiring to run for the United States Senate. Be that as it may, many women have been introduced into the ranks of the women's liberation movement by Betty Friedan's book. Recommended.

Robin Morgan (ed.)
*Sisterhood Is Powerful*
An Anthology of Writings from the Women's Liberation Movement
Vintage Books, Random House, New York, 1970

This collection of sociological articles, autobiographical notes, poems, excerpts from manifestos, for example, the classic S.C.U.M. (Society for Cutting Up Men), and sundry papers provide a representative cross section of the voluminous literature and rapid growth of the W.L.M. The "book is intended to reflect the wide spectrum of political theory and action in women's liberation." (p. XVIII) It does so, successfully.

Norman Mailer
*The Prisoner of Sex*
Signet, The New American Library, Bergenfield, New York, 1971

Apart from a few sharp thrusts at Kate Millett, the book's sole merit rests on the writer's failure to prove that he is a nonsexist liberal. His book is grist for Millett's mills.

Boston Women's Health Collective
*Our Bodies, Our selves: A Course by and for Women*
Simon & Schuster, New York, 1973

It discusses clearly the functioning of the body, how to properly care for it, and when to ask for medical help. It encourages women to demand "answers and explanations from the people you come in contact with for medical care; . . . and insist on enough information to negotiate the system instead of allowing the system to negotiate you."

*Ms.*
Ms. Magazine Corp.
370 Lexington Avenue
New York, N.Y. 10017

Gloria Steinem's slick but uncompromising magazine is good reading for the novice to deeply committed but nonfanatic men or women interested in raising their levels of consciousness.

For an extended list of women's liberation movement literature write to:

Women's Liberation
c/o Wolfson
1520 New Hampshire, N.W.
Washington, D.C. 20036

Women's liberation movement contacts:

National Organization for Women (Now)
P.O. Box 114, Cathedral Station
New York, N.Y. 10025

New York Radical Feminists
P.O. Box 621, Chelsea Station
New York, N.Y. 10011

Black Women's Liberation Committee
346 West 20th Street
New York, N.Y. 10011

# Author-Title Index

# About the Author

Combining a broad background as a group leader and practicing psychiatrist, Thomas R. Verny was born in 1936 in Czechoslovakia and moved to Canada in 1952. He was a teaching fellow at Harvard and Senior Resident in Psychiatry at Massachusetts General Hospital in 1965–1966. In 1966–1967 he taught in the Department of Psychiatry at the University of Toronto. He is presently in private practice in psychiatry and is Program Director for Education and Growth Opportunities at York University. He lives in Toronto with his wife and two children.

Catalog

If you are interested in a list of fine Paperback
books, covering a wide range of subjects
and interests, send your name and address,
requesting your free catalog, to:

McGraw-Hill Paperbacks
1221 Avenue of Americas
New York, N.Y. 10020